EXERCISES

IN

MELODY - WRITING

A SYSTEMATIC COURSE OF MELODIC COMPOSITION, DESIGNED
FOR THE USE OF YOUNG MUSIC STUDENTS,
CHIEFLY AS A COURSE OF EXERCISE COLLATERAL WITH
THE STUDY OF HARMONY

BY

PERCY GOETSCHIUS, Mus. Doc.

(Royal Wurtemberg Professor)

Author of

"THE MATERIAL USED IN MUSICAL COMPOSITION"
"THE THEORY AND PRACTICE OF TONE RELATIONS"
"THE HOMOPHONIC FORMS OF MUSICAL COMPOSITION"
"MODELS OF THE PRINCIPAL MUSICAL FORMS," ETC

NEW YORK
G. SCHIRMER

Copyright, 1900, by G. Schirmer

15209

PREFACE

I.

The object of this course of musical discipline is, to assist the young student (whether or not he expects to become a composer) to form and to cultivate habits of correct melodic thought.

It is simply a carefully graded course of exercise in *melody-invention*,—not conception. The agencies which conduce to the transition from the former into the latter are touched upon in paragraphs 125 to 129, which may be briefly scanned, here, without harm.

The reasons for urging such a course of technical practice upon students of music (general, as well as special students) are two-fold:

1st, because *the prime object of all theoretical study in music is, or should be, melody*. A thorough apprehension of the conditions of correct melody, and command of its natural laws, pave the way to the full and easy reception of all other phases of discipline in music; they are the only natural preparation for successful studies in sight-reading, harmony, counterpoint, form, instrumentation and interpretation.

2nd, because all musical practice, productive or reproductive, in common with all other operations of mind and body, is *the result of habit*, and is therefore qualified exactly according to the quality and energy of the habits which have been contracted, by accident or intention, in early life. The effort to control the formation of these habits, and guide them as early as possible into proper channels, is therefore obviously the most valuable that a wise educational purpose can induce.

Whether there *are* laws governing melodic conduct, or not, is a question to which an answer will be found in the book itself.

II.

It is to be inferred from the above, that the best results will be gained by beginning this course of exercise early in life. Not, however, as a rule, before the twelfth or thirteenth year.

It may be pursued before Harmony is taken up, or entirely independent of the latter. But it will probably prove most efficient as collateral study, *interlined between the exercises of any standard text-book on Harmony;* either from the beginning, or in the later course of harmonic study; in regular alternation with chapters of the latter, or interlined strictly according to subjects.

The degree of benefit to be derived, is manifestly proportionate to the degree of thoroughness with which each lesson is exercised,—precisely as proficiency in scales or any other item of pianoforte technique depends upon the number of times each movement is thoughtfully repeated. It is a system of drill, which must be persisted in until its aim,—*the fixing of habits,*—is achieved. For this reason, the course should cover a full year.

The musical illustrations have been made unusually copious, because this particular phase of musical education is likely to be absorbed by the pupil quite as readily through sensuous contact with melodic sounds, as by mental induction. Therefore, they are to be studied as faithfully as the text, **both at, and away from,** the key-board.

PERCY GOETSCHIUS, Mus. Doc

Boston, Mass.
September, 1893.

EXERCISES IN MELODY-WRITING.

DIVISION ONE.
ESSENTIAL TONES.

CHAPTER I.

MAJOR. THE SCALE-LINE, REGULAR

1. Any series of single tones is a Melody. The quality of the melody depends upon the choice and duration of each successive tone. The general conditions of good melody are:

> Coherency, throughout each chain of three or four successive tones;
> Unity, in the design and effect of the complete melodic sentence; and
> Interesting movements, exhibiting sufficient variety to banish every trace of monotony.

2. The choice of successive tones (aside from the question of durations) is subject, fundamentally, to two Primary Rules of melodic movement

FIRST PRIMARY RULE.

3. *A melody may follow the line of the*

MAJOR SCALE,

upward or downward, with almost unlimited freedom.

This yields the smooth species of movement called diatonic, conjunct, or step-wise progression.

EXERCISES IN MELODY-WRITING.

4. Step-wise progressions are regular, and consequently invariably permissible, when they confirm the *natural or inherent melodic inclination of the so-called Active scale-steps* (par. 6).

5. The seven steps of every scale are divided into two classes:

The 1st, 3rd and 5th scale-steps (those which constitute the Tonic Triad, or harmonic core of the key, see par. 18) are *Inactive*. They occupy the centre of harmonic repose, and are therefore inert, not moving except in obedience to some outward impulse.

The others,—the 7th, 6th, 4th and 2nd scale-steps, are *Active*, because they lie outside of this circle of harmonic repose, and are urged by their inherent impulse to regain the condition of rest. For illustration:

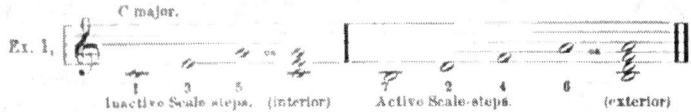

6. The direction, and the degree of urgency, of the movement are dictated by the location of each Active scale-step, and its proximity to the nearest inactive or central scale-step,—as follows:

(a) The tendency is most urgent in the **7th** scale-step, and its direction is *upward*.

(b) The tendency is somewhat less urgent in the **6th** step, and its direction is *downward*.

(c) Still less urgent in the **4th** step,—tendency also *downward*.

(d) The inclination of the 2nd scale-step is evenly balanced between the 1st and 3rd steps, from which it is (practically) equally distant. For that reason it need not be considered in this connection.

For illustration:

7. The progression of an Active scale-step in the proper direction is called its Resolution.

General illustrations:

See also, Ex. 5; Ex. 18, No. 3; Ex. 36, No. 12; Ex. 50.

THE 4-MEASURE PHRASE.

8. The smallest complete melodic sentence, called the Phrase, generally embraces four ordinary measures.

(a) When regular, it begins with one of the (inactive) tones which constitute the Tonic Triad. These may be placed upon the first (accented) beat of the first measure; or one, perhaps more, beats *before* the first full measure. If the Phrase begins, thus, with one or more preliminary tones, their value is to be subtracted from the final measure.

(b) The Phrase closes with the Tonic (i. e., the key-note); upon an *accented* beat of the fourth measure (upon either accent, if a compound measure); and preceded by either of the three tones which constitute the Dominant Triad (see par. 19). This ending is called the Perfect Cadence.

Thus (in C-major):

1. Triple rhythm.

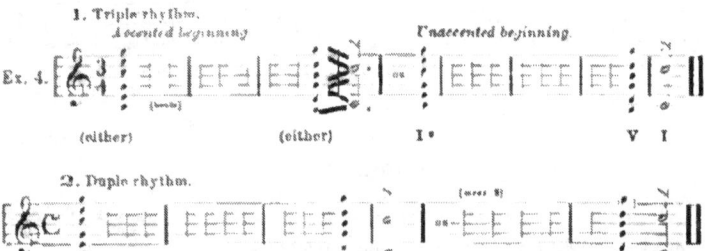

2. Duple rhythm.

* These chord names are explained in Chap. III, par. 18, 19.

9. Besides the step-wise progressions, up or down the line of the major scale according to the first Primary Rule, it is everywhere permissible

(*a*) To *repeat a tone*, once or oftener. For example:

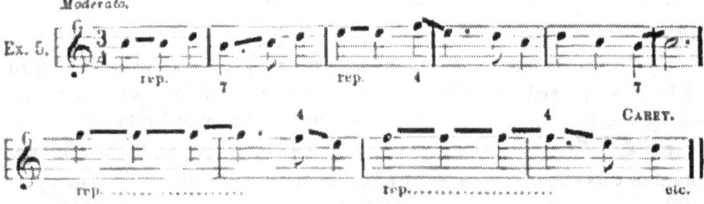

See also Ex. 3, Nos. 5 and 6; Ex. 32, No. 3; Ex. 36, Nos. 1, 8, 9; Ex. 54.

(*b*) To *progress upward or downward by the interval of a third,* i. e., overleaping one diatonic scale-step. If this skip of a third is made from an Inactive tone, it involves no obligation whatever. If made from an Active scale-step (namely, from the 7th, 6th or 4th,—as stated in par. 6 *d*, the 2nd scale-step is not subject to *any* of the rules of active steps), the consequences depend upon the direction of the leap. No subsequent consideration is necessary if the melody makes the leap in the proper direction (from the 7th scale-step upward, from the 6th or 4th step downward, as is to be done in the present lesson). For illustration:

A. From Inactive tones.

B. From Active tones, in the proper direction

7   6   4   (par. 38 b.)

LESSON 1.

A number of original melodies (at least one in each key), with *strict* regard to the following limitations and directions.

(1) Only in major keys

(2) Without modulations,—i. e., each melody in one key throughout.

(3) As 4-measure Phrases, according to the models of Ex 4

(4) In 2/2, 2/4, 3/2, 3/4, 3/8, 4/4, 4/8, 6/8, and 6/4-measure, successively

(5) The rhythm strictly uniform, i. e., one tone to each beat, as ♩, ♪ or ♩, according to the chosen measure,—excepting the final cadence-tone (see Ex. 4)

(6) The scale-line, tone-repetitions, and an occasional skip of a third are to be employed. Of the latter, only one at a time (perhaps returning, as shown in Ex 6),—not two successive leaps in the same direction.

(7) No violation of the natural tendency of Active scale-steps is permitted in this lesson. Each is to move in the proper *direction*. Examples 2 and 6 b.

NOTE —The work should be, at present, merely the *mechanical* application of the given rules; these rules are to become *habits*,—formed and established, as habits are, by persistent systematic effort. After regular, correct melodic movement has become a habit of thought, the tones will soon invest themselves, more or less unconsciously, with feeling and purpose, and all exceptional progressions will be likely to rectify or justify themselves.

At the same time, the student *must endeavor to hear each tone* as he writes it down, without the aid of an instrument, and must not desist until he can thus mentally follow, accurately, every melodic movement. Further, each melody, when completed, must be *sung* and then tested at the key-board,—but not until *completed*; the invention must be prosecuted away from any instrument.

CHAPTER II.

THE SCALE-LINE, EXCEPTIONAL.

10. It is always possible to evade the Resolution, i. e., to counteract the natural tendency, of the three Active scale-steps, and force them to progress in the opposite direction, by approaching them, along the line of the scale, in the corresponding (i. e., opposite) direction. This confirms the first Primary Rule, in its fullest sense. For example:

See also Ex. 47, No. 1; Ex. 52, No. 2.

11. If approached in the direction of their Resolution, along the scale, however, the natural inclination is reinforced, and *must* be fulfilled,—at present. Thus:

* Somewhat less objectionable, because the tendency of the 4th scale-step is less urgent than that of the other Active tones (par. 6 c).

In other words, the melody, in pursuing the line of the scale *upward*, may turn back (if desired) at any point excepting the 7th scale-step; in pursuing the line of the scale *downward*, it can turn at any point excepting the 6th or 4th step.

12. As intimated in par. 9 b, the skip of a third may be made in either direction, even from an Active scale-step. An obligation is involved only when the leap of a third is made contrary to the natural tendency of the Active tone; in which case the melody must immediately *turn back*,—either by a leap, to the preceding tone, or by step-wise progression. For illustration:

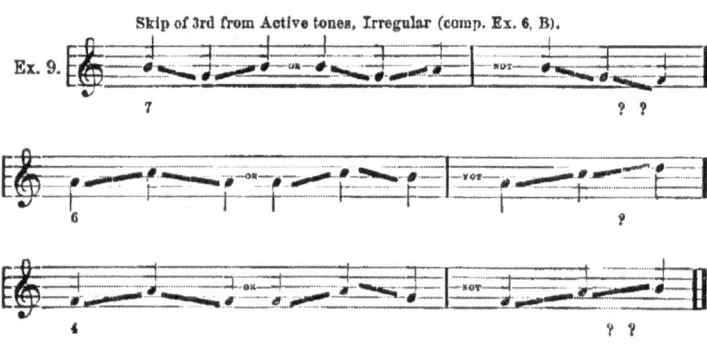

LESSON 2.

A number of original 4-measure melodies (at least one in each major key), according to all the directions of the preceding lesson, excepting (7); both the regular and irregular progressions of the Active scale-steps are to be employed. The danger of *monotony*, arising from the uniformity of rhythm, must be counteracted by variety of tone-succession; avoid moving about in the *narrow compass* of the same 3 or 4 tones, and, as a rule, avoid returning too frequently to the same tone, especially on corresponding beats of consecutive measures.

CHAPTER III.

THE CHORD-LINE.

SECOND PRIMARY RULE.

13. *A melody may follow the line of any good* **CHORD** *upward or downward, with almost unlimited freedom.*

This yields the more vigorous species of movement called disjunct, or by skip (or leap); and affords the necessary contrast with the step-wise progressions.

14. The "Scale-line" may be abandoned for the "Chord-line," or the chord-line for the scale-line, at any point in a melody,—subject to a few self-evident restrictions.

15. The influence of HARMONY (i. e., the construction, relation and succession of CHORDS) upon melody-formation is so great and constant, that this is probably the most vital of the two Primary Rules. Unless already familiar with the elementary conditions of Harmony, the pupil must study the following brief exposition so thoroughly, and transfer all illustrations to every other key so frequently and perseveringly, as to acquire absolute freedom in recognizing and employing the principal chord-lines correctly.

16. The tones which constitute a chord are found by adding one higher 3rd after another, to the fundamental tone which is to be the *root*, and the index of the chord (of its name, quality, and relation to other chords). Thus, for the "chord of C":

Ex. 10.

chord-root, chord-third, chord-fifth. c-e-g.

These letters, *c-e-g*, constitute the chord of *c*; and they may appear as representatives of that chord-line *in any order.* Thus:

Ex. 11.

c - e - g   e - g - c   g - e - c   etc., etc.

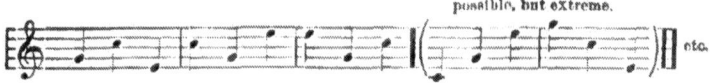

FUNDAMENTAL HARMONIC PRINCIPLES.

17. Each key comprises three classes or families of chords, called respectively the

> *Tonic* class;
> *Dominant* class; and
> *Second-Dominant* or *Sub-Dominant* class.

18. The TONIC CLASS consists of two chords, one erected upon the *first* scale-step, or Tonic note, and called the *Tonic Triad* or *"The One"* (marked I); and one of subordinate rank erected upon the *sixth* scale-step, and called *"The Six"* (marked VI); the latter is much less common than the I. These Tonic chords are limited to three Tones,—hence their title "Triad." Thus, in C-major:

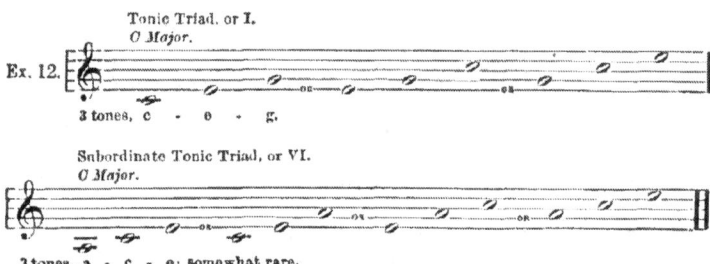

19. *(a)* The DOMINANT CLASS consists of a cluster of chords erected upon the *fifth* scale-step, or Dominant. These chords may embrace as many as five tones, the lowermost of which (the root) is often omitted. They are erected and named as follows in C-major:

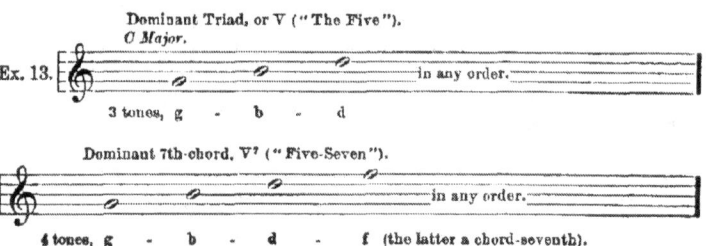

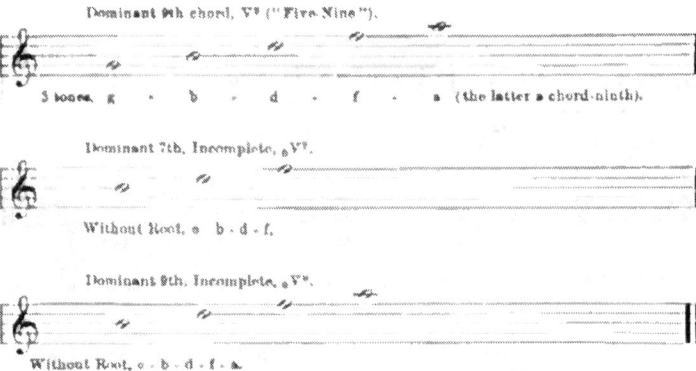

(b) To the Dominant class belongs also a Triad of subordinate rank, erected upon the *third* scale-step (the III); it is so rare and unimportant that it may be ignored altogether in connection with melody-invention,— i. e., it is not a "good" chord (par. 13).

20. The SECOND-DOMINANT or SUB-DOMINANT class consists of a cluster of chords erected upon the *second* scale-step, in precisely the same manner as those on the Dominant,—containing five tones, with *frequent* omissions of the root. Thus, in C-major:

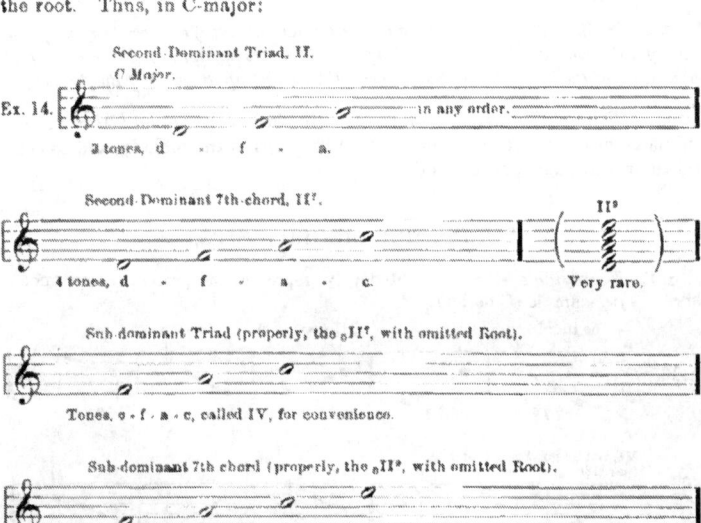

EXERCISES IN MELODY-WRITING.

Summary (C-major):

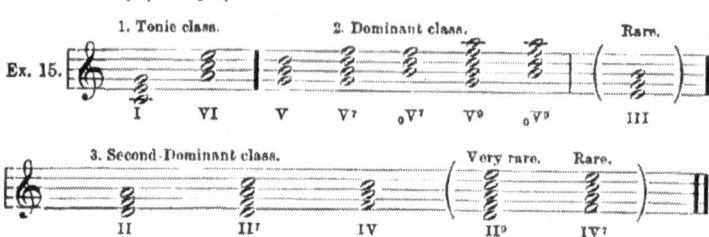

N. B.—This table must be reproduced in every major key, daily for a time, at the key-board, and in writing.

21. The few primary rules which govern the succession, or movements, of these chord-classes are as follows:

(a) The chords of the Tonic class may progress into (i. e., may be followed by) *any other* chord of the same key.

(b) The chords of the Dominant class can only progress easily into those of the Tonic class, preferably into the I, more rarely into the VI. The progression of a Dominant chord into one of the Second-Dominant class is uncommon, and need not be considered in melody-invention.

(c) The chords of the Second-Dominant class pass most readily into those of the Dominant class; but they may also be followed by those of the Tonic.

22. N. B.—*These rules of chord-succession are so fully confirmed by the rules of inherent melodic tendency (explained in paragraphs 4-6), that careful observance of the latter facilitates, largely, the correct application of the former.*

23. Nevertheless, it is necessary to be fully conscious of the quality and name of the chord-lines represented by skips in the melody, and to control their movements accordingly.

RULES FOR SINGLE SKIPS.

24. Each *single* skip must obviously represent, at present, some good chord. For example (C-major):

25. With this single limitation, a leap may be made from any tone, Active or Inactive, upward or downward. The rule of inherent melodic tendencies, or Resolutions (par. 6) is, consequently, not binding upon the Active scale-steps during skips that constitute good chord-lines. While it is *always smoother and more natural to conduct these scale-steps in the proper direction*, they may *leap* along a good chord-line, without objection, in the opposite direction,—even irrespective of the manner in which they are approached (par. 11). Thus:

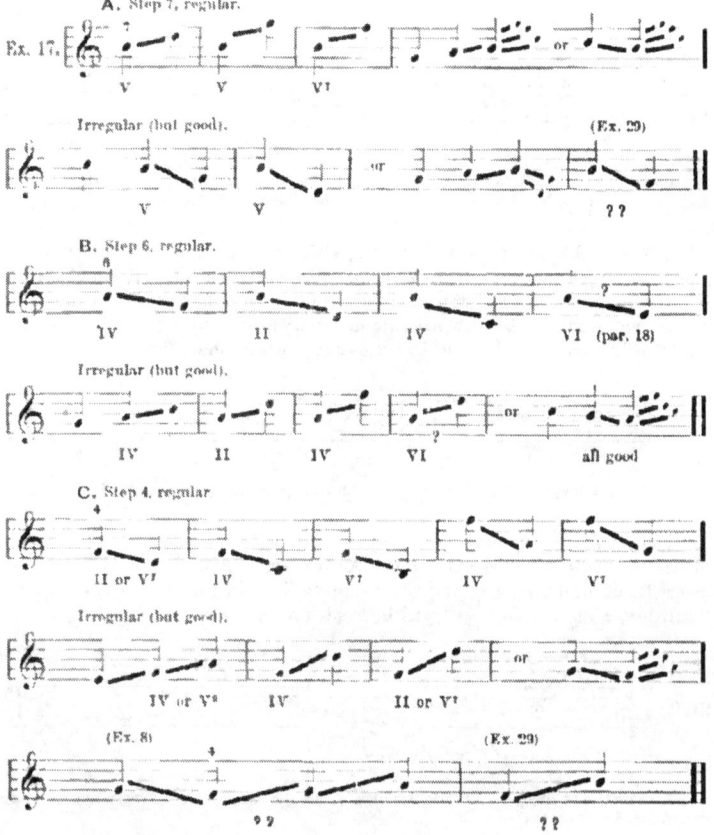

26. The leap of a *Third* (called a "narrow" skip), as has been seen, is always permissible. Any larger leaps than this (called "wide" skips) are subject to the following general condition:

After a wide skip (i. e., any distance beyond a third) *the melody is very likely to turn*, and progress, by scale or chord-line, in the opposite direction. Thus:

See also, Ex. 32, No. 1; Ex. 36, Nos. 4, 14, 18, 19, 20; Ex. 52, No. 5; Ex. 60, No. 2; Ex. 64, No. 3; Ex. 75, Nos. 1, 2; Ex. 100, No. 3; Ex. 101, No. 5; Ex. 117, Nos. 11, 12.

27. *(a)* If the melody, however, violates this rule, by continuing in the *same* direction after a wide skip *along the line of the scale*, it should, as a rule, pass on only one step, and *then* turn. In other words, while it is always more natural to turn back immediately after a wide leap, it is usually sufficiently correct to do so at the *second* following tone. Thus:

*1) From *d* down to either of these tones.   *2) From *f* to either of these.   *3) To either.

(b) At the same time, if the scale-tone that follows the skip in the same direction chances to be one of the Active tones, it is more than likely to assert its natural tendency and resolve properly,—in which case the rule of "turning, after a wide leap" will be evaded altogether. Thus:

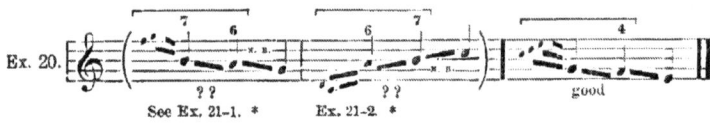

* These two progressions are doubtful in any case, for they involve a violation of both the rule of par. 6 *a*, and that of par. 26.

28. *(a)* The rule of par. 26 gives emphasis to the still more binding and important rule, that

It is possible to skip to any Active tone in the direction *opposite to the tendency* of the latter, namely: *from any tone* (though seldom beyond an octave) *downward to the 7th scale-step;* from any tone *upward* to the *6th* or *4th* scale-step, — because their natural Resolution provides for the change of direction after the leap. Thus:

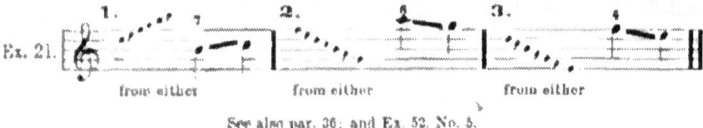

Ex. 21.
from either   from either   from either

See also par. 36; and Ex. 52, No. 5.

(b) It must not be inferred, however, that this is necessary. It is of course also possible, though far less regular, to leap upon an Active tone in the other direction (i. e., *upward* to the 7th scale-step, and *downward* to the *6th* or *4th* step), though only along some perfectly good chord-line, as already seen (par. 24).

29. *(a)* If the Active tones are approached by a wide leap irregularly (in the direction *corresponding* to their Resolution: up to the 7th, down to the 6th or 4th steps), it will either afford an additional opportunity of obtaining the irregular progressions given in par. 10 (Ex. 7), in keeping with the rule of par. 26 ("turning, after a wide skip"); thus:

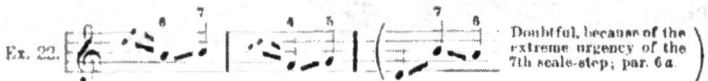

Ex. 22.
Doubtful, because of the extreme urgency of the 7th scale-step; par. 6 a.

(b) Or, better, it will be found expedient to take advantage of the license of par. 27 a,—i. e., to turn back at the *second* following tone. Thus:

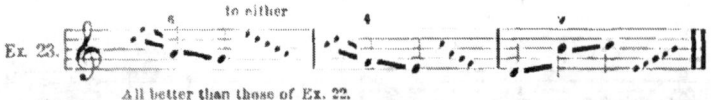

Ex. 23.
to either

All better than those of Ex. 22.

30. The leap of an *octave* is allowed from any tone, upward or downward (according to the low or high pitch of the tone from which the leap is to be made). This is simply a wider version of par. 9 a. For illustration:

par. 26.   par. 27 a.

Ex. 24.
to either

LESSON 3.

A large number of original 4-measure Melodies, in all major keys, and in all the species of measure prescribed in Lesson 1. The rhythm uniform. The scale-line and skips of a 3rd to be used as before; and, besides these, *single wide skips* (i. e., each wide skip followed by the scale-line, or by a narrow leap) may occur, according to the above rules. Sing, and play, each melody *when completed*.

CHAPTER IV.

THE CHORD-LINE, CONTINUED.

31. Review par. 13, and Ex. 11. If the melody is to continue, after a wide skip, with *another skip in the same direction* (contrary to the general principle of par. 26), it may pass into *any tone which harmonizes with the tones of the preceding skip*,—and so on, as far as the skips extend in the same direction. This rule represents simply the application of the second Primary Rule (par. 13) in a broader sense. For example:

32. If the last tone of the faulty groups (faulty, because the last tone does not harmonize with the preceding tones) be desired, it may *always* be reached by *turning*,—i. e., it may be taken in a higher, or lower, octave-register. Thus:

33. This important rule appears to have some bearing upon a single skip which follows after the scale-line *in the same direction;* it is always best to skip thus onward to some tone which bears obvious affinity to the *ruling harmonic impression* of the preceding scale-tones. What this ruling impression is, depends chiefly upon the location of the accent. For illustration:

34. The repetition of a tone (par. 9 *a*) arrests, to a certain extent, the operation of the rules of the skip (par. 26 and 31). Thus:

35. The most objectionable progression is, probably, that of the augmented fourth,—formed in major by the leap from the 4th scale-step *up to*

the 7th step, and vice versa, from the 7th scale-step *down* to the 4th step. Thus:

This progression is checked, in each case, both by par. 6 (the inherent tendency of the first tone), and by par. 28 *b* (the irregular leap to an Active tone). It is, however, possible to justify it as derivation from the line of the Incomplete Dominant-7th chord (Ex. 13), if it is an *entirely obvious* image of the chord-line. Thus:

36. The skip of a seventh is only advisable when it occurs either in keeping with par. 28 *a*; or as derivative of the Dominant-7th chord-line. Thus:

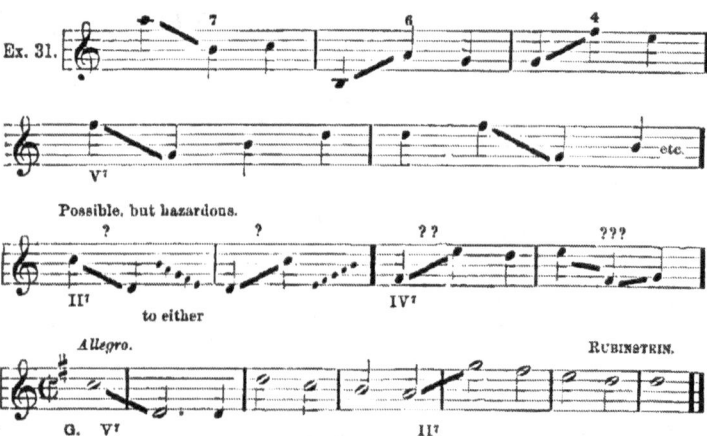

37. A succession of skips describing the line of some chord (as in Ex. 11), should, as a general rule, *coincide in extent with the fundamental rhythmic groups*, i. e., embracing in duple measure 2, 4 or 8 beats, in triple measure 3, 6, 9 or 12 beats. In this way the *chord*-images will confirm, and even serve to indicate, the *rhythmic* design. In other words, the chord-line extends, usually, only to the end of a rhythmic group (through a half measure or whole measure) and is then exchanged, at the following *accent*, either for a new chord-line, or for the scale-line. It must be understood that this, however, is only a *general* rule, subject to many obvious modifications. For illustration:

See also, Ex. 36, No. 10; Ex. 52, No. 6; Ex 61, No. 2.

38. All melodic formations of four consecutive tones, to which the above rules of the skip do not appear to extend, must be controlled by the regulations of *chord-succession*; for there are many places in a melody where the influence which Harmony exerts over melody is peculiarly manifest (par. 15), especially when the location of the *accented* tones is considered. Among these formations may be classed:

(a) Certain successions of skips in opposite directions. For example:

(b) The *interception* of the Resolution of Active scale-steps (par. 7) by interposing an *unaccented* tone between the Active tone and its resolving tone. Here, the location of the tones in the measure is of dominating importance, as no other than unaccented tones can safely be inserted. If two tones are interposed, the Resolution *may* be evaded altogther. For example:

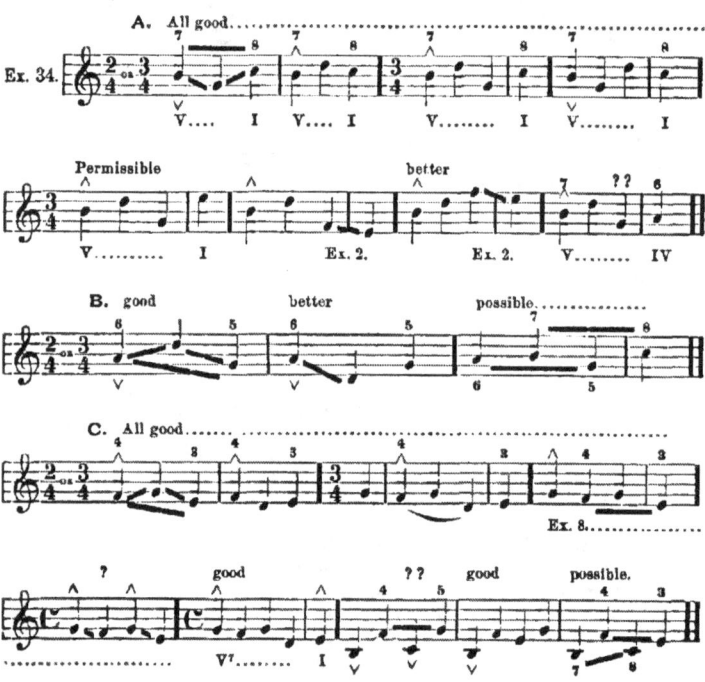

24   EXERCISES IN MELODY-WRITING.

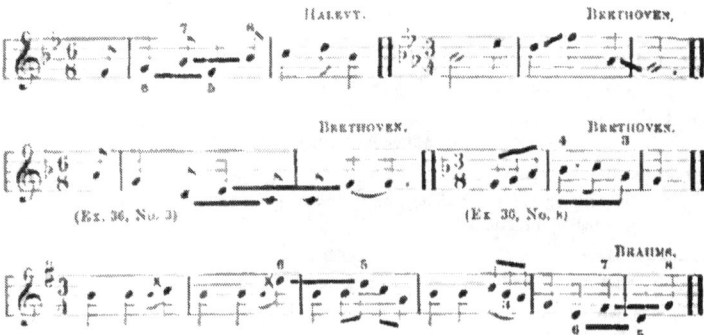

(c) Successive wide leaps which represent the *alternate presentation* of the tones of *two different* (contiguous) melody-lines. Thus:

See also, Ex. 52, No. 6; Ex. 62, No. 6; Ex. 95, No. 5; Ex. 117, Nos. 7, 8.

39. *N. B.*—Pupils who are not yet sufficiently familiar with the chords and the rules of chord-succession, are likely to find these minuter distinctions confusing. If so, they may omit this last paragraph,—or any other troublesome paragraphs,—for a time, with perfect safety. *Such confusion can only arise from the use of the irregular and exceptional phases of melodic treatment.* If the student will avoid these, and limit himself for awhile to the strict observance of the *fundamental rules*, and the *regular* modes of melodic conduct, he can encounter no difficulty or embarrassment: namely, the two Primary Rules, paragraphs 3 and 13,—

    Movement along the Scale-line or Chord-line'

and, besides these, paragraph 4,—

    Proper Resolution of the Active Scale-steps;

paragraph 10,—

    Overcoming natural tendency, by approaching the tone, along the scale, in corresponding direction;

paragraph 24,—

    Each single skip representing some good Chord-line;

paragraph 26,—

    Changing the direction, after a wide leap;

paragraph 28 *a*,—

    Approaching an Active tone in the direction opposite to that of its Resolution;

and paragraph 31,—

    Successive leaps in same direction representing a good collective chord-effect.

These few rules practically suffice for primary melodic conduct, and, once firmly established in the mind of the pupil, as *habits* of melodic thought, all exceptional and irregular forms of melodic succession will be found to follow as a matter of course, and regulate themselves, sooner or later.

    Additional miscellaneous illustrations of all the foregoing chapters; the figures in parenthesis refer to paragraphs:

EXERCISES IN MELODY-WRITING. 27

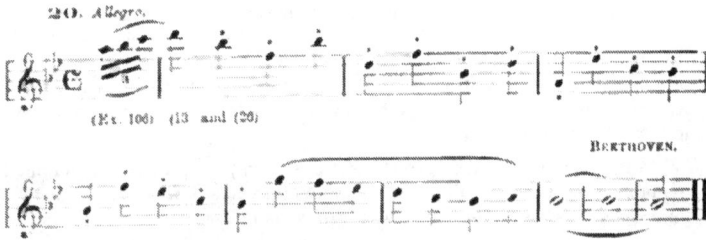

See also, Ex. 96, Nos. 1, 2; — and examine "TONE-RELATIONS" (G. Schirmer, N. Y., 1900), Lesson 10, all; Lesson 13, all; Lesson 24, Nos. 2, 3 and 5.

LESSON 4.

A large number of 4-measure melodies, in all major keys, and in all the species of Measure prescribed in Lesson 1. The rhythm uniform. The scale-line and chord-lines to be employed, in the most comprehensive manner, according to the given directions. Recollect, and apply freely, par. 9 a and par. 30. Review the note to Lesson 1; and par. 39, thoroughly.

Sing, and play, each melody when completed.

Such melodies of these first 4 Lessons as have been corrected and approved by the teacher, may be *harmonized*, by those students whose knowledge of Harmony enables them to perform the task successfully.

CHAPTER V.

MINOR.

40. The true minor mode, that is, the *harmonic* form, corresponds to the major scale of the same key-note, excepting that the *6th and 3d scale-steps are lowered* a chromatic half-step. Thus:

All melodic and harmonic movements in minor are regulated upon the basis of *this*, the *harmonic*, form of the scale. Before proceeding farther, the student must familiarize himself *absolutely* with this derivation. Every minor scale must be written out, according to Ex. 37, and played repeatedly. And the table of Ex. 15 is also to be written out in every minor mode (with lowered 3rd and 6th steps).

41. All the Scale-conditions and Chord-conditions of the major mode, explained in the preceding four chapters, are therefore *similarly valid for minor*,—with a few self-evident limitations, as follows:

42. The most noteworthy limitation for minor melodies, is an exception to par. 10, as far as the 6th and 7th scale-steps are concerned. *These should not appear in immediate succession*, as a very general rule. Ex. 7, measures 1 and 2, are therefore only valid in *C-major*,—not in *C-minor* (Ex. 7, measure 3, however, is not involved in this restriction). Thus:

C-minor. The flat is inserted before *a* for greater clearness.

This also affects a portion of Ex. 17, Ex. 20, Ex. 22, and a portion of Ex. 28,—*no others*.

43. This succession is nevertheless possible, though very rare, as *obvious* derivation from the chord-line of the Diminished-7th chord (i. e., the Dominant-9th chord, in the *minor* mode, incomplete,—Ex. 15, chord no. 7, with $a\flat$). Thus:

44. Further,—an additional augmented fourth occurs in minor, formed by leaping from the 6th scale-step *up* to the 2nd step; and vice versa, from the 2nd step *down* to the 6th step. Thus:

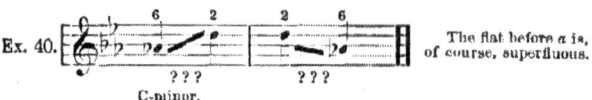

This progression, like that of Ex. 29, is checked either by the irregularity of carrying the 6th scale-step upward (par. 6 *b*), or of leaping down upon it, in the direction of its Resolution (par. 28 *b*).

And, like the former, and like the irregularity of Ex. 38, it is possible to justify it as obvious derivation from a chord-line,—either from that of the Diminished-7th chord ($_0V^9$ in minor), or from the II. Thus:

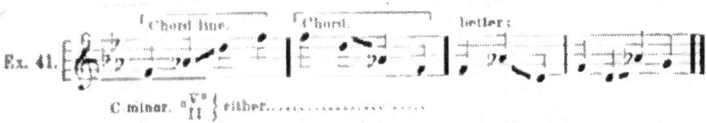

45. Further,—the well-nigh intolerable interval of the augmented fifth occurs, in minor, in leaping from the 3rd scale-step *up* to the 7th step, and vice versa. Thus:

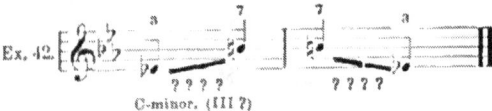

This error is checked by several rules,—par. 24, par. 28 b, par. 6 a.

The leap from step 3 *down* to step 7, on the contrary, is perfectly good (par. 28 a). But the leap from step 7 *up* to step 3 had better be avoided (for the present), as it represents a very improbable chord. For illustration:

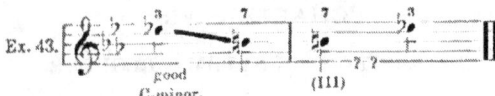

N. B.—*Every musical illustration given in Chapters I to IV is to be reviewed and tested in the corresponding minor key* (explained in Ex. 37).

Additional general illustrations:

EXERCISES IN MELODY-WRITING. 31

See also, Ex. 55, No. 3; Ex. 63, No. 8; Ex. 65, No. 1; Ex. 129, Nos. 5, 6;—and "TONE-RELATIONS," Lesson 11, all; 16, No. 7; 18, No. 7; 21, No. 4; 22, No. 4.

LESSON 5.

A large number of 4-measure melodies, in all the MINOR keys, and all the species of Measure prescribed in Lesson 1. Rhythm uniform. All details precisely as in Lesson 4. *Avoid monotony.*

CHAPTER VI.

DIVERSITY OF RHYTHM. REGULAR.

46. The rhythmic effect of a melody may be heightened by employing tones of *different time-values* (instead of uniform beats, as in the preceding chapters).

(a) The disposition of these values is *Regular,*

When the comparatively *longer* (i. e., heavier) tones occupy the *accented* beats, or accented beat-fractions; and, vice versa, when the comparatively *shorter* (i. e., lighter) tones occupy *unaccented* beats, or beat-fractions. Thus:

[musical examples]

(b) Uniform divisions of an entire measure (i. e., uniform beats, or beat-fractions) are always regular, also, because they do not contradict the above conditions. Thus:

Ex. 46. [musical example]

47. It is generally advisable to avoid using extreme time-values in the same Phrase-melody. For instance, in 2/4 or 4/4 measure, ♩-notes (as sum of two beats) and ♪-notes (as simple division) may both occur;—*occasionally* also a dotted half-note, or a 16th-note; but the whole note would be rare, and 32nd-notes almost out of the question. In other words, the beats indicated in the signature should constitute the fundamental or average time-value; this may be augmented by one or two (rarely three) *additions*, or diminished by one or two *divisions*.

The melodies given in Exs. 3, 7, 32 (excepting Nos. 1 and 5), 34 and 36 (excepting Nos. 10, 11) are all constructed in regular rhythm. They are to be carefully reviewed, from this standpoint. See also, "TONE-RELATIONS," Lesson 18, Nos. 1, 4, 5, 8; 22, Nos. 1, 2, 6; 30, Nos. 1, 4.

48. Rhythmic diversity is derived from *uniform* rhythm by the following methods:

(a) By employing the dot;

[musical example]

(b) By any other process of lengthening one or more of the original tones;

[musical example]

Further, diversity is procured—

(c) By placing *less* or *more* tones in a measure than the number of its

fundamental beats; for instance, in 3/4 measure, less or more than three tones. The first gives addition, the other gives division, of beats. Thus:

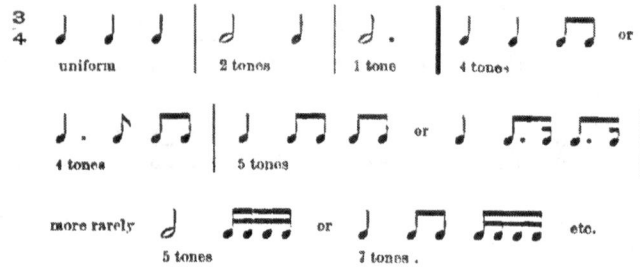

The "triplet" will be regarded, at present, as 6/8 or 9/8 Measure.

49. *Rests* represent, commonly, the suppression of a portion of one of the original tones;—generally an *unaccented* fraction, in which case the Rest *follows* the tone; sometimes, however, an *accented* fraction, in which case the Rest *precedes* the tone which it represents, and as the equivalent of which it is to be treated. For illustration (the slurs indicate which tones the rests are borrowed from):

See also, Ex. 56, No. 2; Ex. 59, No. 3; Ex. 87, No. 2; Ex. 95, No. 4; Ex. 102, No. 3; Ex. 106, No. 5; Ex. 117, No. 9.

The employment of rests (which must be very sparing, at present) is subject to no other rule than that they must never be permitted to sever the continuity of the Melody; if used under conditions that preserve or restore the coherency, or perhaps even emphasize the structural unity of the sentence, they are certain to be permissible and effective.

LESSON 6.

A. Take a number of the melodies invented in preceding lessons, in uniform rhythm, and diversify the rhythm in *regular* forms according to par 48 *a* and *b* (without altering the number of tones in the original form)

B. Invent a large number of new melodies with diversified rhythm, *regular*, as shown in par. 48 *a*, *b* and *c*. A *very few* rests may be inserted.

Employ every species of Measure prescribed in Lesson I; and write *alternately in the major and minor mode.*

Be careful to make all shorter tones *essential* (see par. 100).

LESSON 7.

A number of four-measure melodies in 9/8, 9/4 and 12/8 Measure. Rhythm diversified, *regular* forms, different major and minor keys, alternately.

Such melodies of these two lessons as have been corrected and approved by the teacher, may be harmonized, by pupils in Harmony.

CHAPTER VII.

THE PERIOD-FORM.

50. The "Period" generally embraces 8 measures; that is, *two phrases*, of 4 measures each The first of these is called the Antecedent, the second one the Consequent Phrase

51. *(a)* The Antecedent Phrase begins exactly like any single Phrase, according to par 8 *a*. But it ends, not with the Perfect cadence (8 *b*), but with a so-called Semicadence,—upon an accented beat of the 4th measure, *with either one of the three tones which compose the Dominant Triad.*

(b) The Consequent Phrase follows, usually beginning on the *same beat* with which the Antecedent began, and ending, like any single Phrase, with

the Perfect cadence,—upon an accented beat of the final (8th) measure, with the Tonic note. Thus (in C-major):

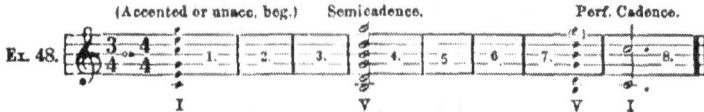

52. In the first few examples invented, the Consequent Phrase must *correspond to the melody of the Antecedent*, excepting the last 3 or 4 tones; these always differ, because of the diversity of cadence. The formation of such Period-melodies is called "parallel construction." For illustration:

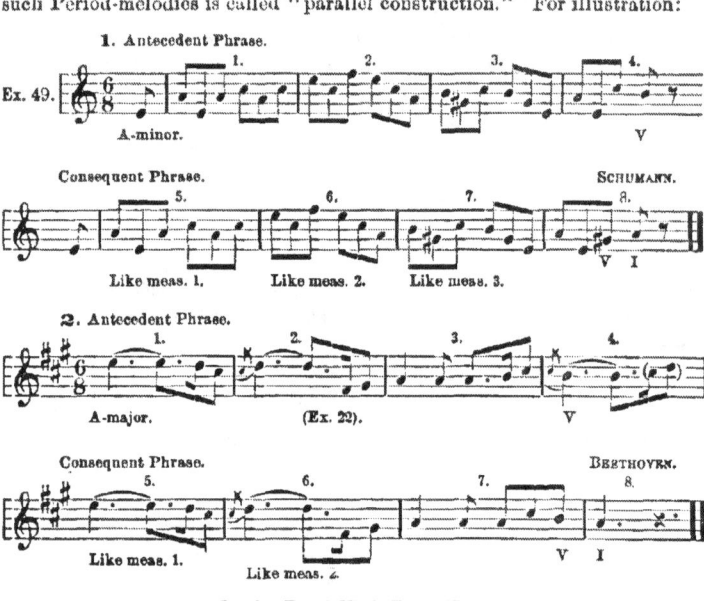

See also, Ex. 52, No. 1; Ex. 53, No. 2.

53. In each succeeding example, the extent of this similarity between the Phrases is to be *diminished gradually*,—more and more tones in measure 7, then 6, and then 5, are to differ from those of measure 3, then 2, and then 1; until, finally, the entire Consequent Phrase is independent of its Antecedent. This ultimate formation is called the Period of "contrasting construction." Thus:

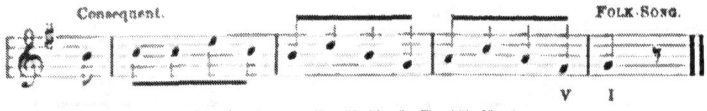

See also, Ex. 54, Ex 55, No. 2; Ex 129, No. 1.

The appropriateness of a brief Rest *at the cadences* is demonstrated in both of these examples (49 and 50); see par. 49.

LESSON 8.

A large number of 8-measure melodies, in Period-form, according to par. 51; at first, several in parallel construction (par. 52), and then gradually more and more contrasting (par. 53).

Rhythm diversified (but regular); all the species of Measure prescribed in Lesson 1; different major and minor keys, alternately. An *occasional* rest may be inserted, chiefly at (after) the semicadence.

Review the note to Lesson 1; and par. 39. *Avoid monotony.* Sing, and then play, each melody, when completed.

After correction, some of these Period-melodies may be harmonized. Where the construction is parallel, the *harmonization* of the Consequent may differ from that of the (melodically similar) Antecedent.

CHAPTER VIII.

IRREGULAR RHYTHM.

54. Review par. 46 a, thoroughly.

The disposition of various time-values is *Irregular,* when the conditions of Regular rhythm are violated, namely,

When the *heavier* (comparatively longer) tones in a measure occupy comparatively *light* beats or beat-fractions of that measure; and, vice versa, when the *lighter* tones (brief, subdivisions of beats) occupy comparatively *heavier* pulses in the group.

For illustration (the *regular* forms, Ex. 45, are here repeated, for comparison):

Ex. 51. (a) 2/4 [musical notation] regular.... irregular....

[musical notation] regular.... irregular.... regular....

[musical notation] irregular....

[musical notation] regular.... irregular.... regular....

[musical notation] etc.
slightly irregular.... irregular....

(b) 3/4 [musical notation] regular....

[musical notation] irregular....

[musical notation] etc.

(c) 4/4 [musical notation] etc., as in 2/4 [musical notation]
regular.... slightly irreg.....

[musical notation] etc.
irregular....

(d) 6/8 [musical notation] etc. [musical notation]
regular.... irregular....

[musical notation] etc.

In other words: if the tone upon the first beat (or any other *accent*) is *longer* than, or at least *as long* as, any other tone in the same group (measure), the rhythmic disposition is Regular,—otherwise Irregular.

55. The degree of irregularity depends, of course, upon the degree of discrepancy between the length of the tone and the comparative dynamic quality, or length, of the beat or beat-fraction upon which the tone is misplaced. For instance, upon a pulse entitled to an 8th-note only, it is more irregular to locate a ♩-note, than a ♪-note. In Ex. 51 c, measure 5 is more irregular than measure 6, or measures 3 and 4.

56. (*a*) Irregular rhythmic figures are never objectionable, *excepting when isolated*, — and not always positively wrong, even then, though usually so. In other words,

An irregular rhythmic figure may always be justified *by recurring;*— either immediately, in the *next* following group or measure; or in some, not unreasonably remote, *corresponding* measure;

namely: measures 1 and 3, or 2 and 4, of the four-measure Phrase; and measures 1 and 5, 2 and 6, 3 and 7, or 4 and 8 of the eight-measure Period. For example:

EXERCISES IN MELODY-WRITING.

See also, Ex. 36, No. 10; Ex. 54, meas. 6, 7; Ex. 58, No. 5; Ex. 62, Nos. 1 and 2; Ex. 80, No. 2; Ex. 100, Nos. 2, 7; Ex. 117, No. 11; Ex. 129, No. 13.

Examine "TONE-RELATIONS," Lesson 13, No. 4; 16, No. 2; 32, Nos 3 and 4; 35, No. 3.

(b) Illustrations of a very common rhythmic irregularity in *triple* measure, which appears to demand no justification (♪♩ ♩ ♩), are found in Ex. 32, No. 5 (end); Ex. 55, No. 2 (end); Ex. 56, No. 2 (end); etc.

LESSON 9.

A large number of 4-measure and 8-measure melodies, with Irregular rhythmic measures, according to the above rules,—particularly par. 56. It will be well to limit this exercise to *occasional* rhythmic irregularities, introduced in Phrases or Periods of an otherwise regular and simple design. *Extreme* irregularities (par. 55) should be avoided.

Use the varieties of Measure prescribed in Lesson 1; different major and minor keys, alternately.

At first, experiment with former melodies, modifying their rhythm without altering the tones. Then invent new ones, with immediate reference to Irregular rhythm.

CHAPTER IX.

EXCEPTIONAL SEMICADENCES.

57. The Semicadence, in the center of the Period-form, may be made, somewhat exceptionally, upon *some other than the tones of the Dominant Triad* (prescribed in par. 51 *a*).

Any scale-step of the prevailing key may be chosen, thus to end the Antecedent Phrase; but it is well to avoid the key-note itself, as this is needed for the final (perfect) cadence. For example:

In Ex. 52, No. 5, the cadence of the first Phrase is made upon the Tonic; this is very exceptional, but, of course, possible.

58. Further, the semicadence-tone may occasionally be shifted to the *second* beat of the group, especially in triple measure (3/4, 3/8, 6/8), instead of falling upon an accent (first beat of the group) as prescribed. In this case it should, as a rule, be preceded (on the accent) by the *next higher*, or next lower, scale-step, as obvious grace-note. Thus:

EXERCISES IN MELODY-WRITING. 41

See also, Ex. 36, No. 14; Ex. 57, No. 2; Ex. 58, No. 1.

LESSON 10.

A number of 8-measure melodies in Period-form, with the exceptional forms of semicadence explained above.

CHAPTER X.

SYNTAX OF MELODY.

59. The succession of tones in a Phrase or Period-melody, may be determined by a broader consideration than the application of given rules to each *single* unit of the melodic succession; namely,—by the principle of *symmetrical recurrence*, applied to an entire *group* of consecutive tones.

The recurrence, or reproduction of the group, may assume the form—

(1) Of an exact REPETITION; or
(2) Of a SEQUENCE.

60. The "Repetition" is a literal recurrence, upon the *self-same scale-steps*. Thus:

61. The "Sequence" is a reproduction of the group of tones upon *other scale-steps*, a certain interval-distance above or below the original tones. Thus:

62. The initial group or figure, to be reproduced in either of these ways, may be of almost any length; but it is frequently exactly one measure, and, in any case, it is almost certain *to correspond to the fundamental rhythmic groups*, i. e., to include 2, 4 or 8 beats in duple Measure, and 3, 6, 9 or 12 beats in triple Measure,—similar to the conditions of par. 37 (which review), and for the same reasons. Further, the group may begin upon any beat of the measure. For illustration:

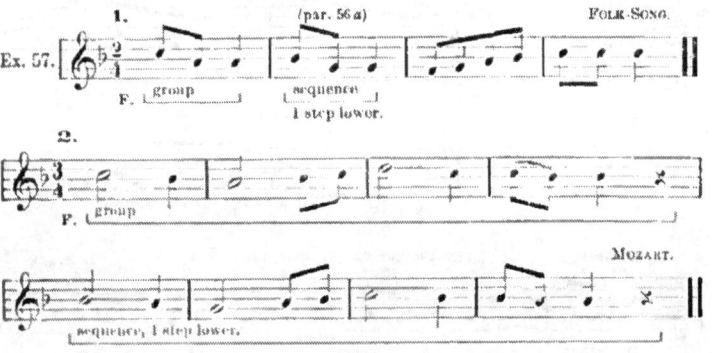

At Ex. 55, No. 1, and Ex. 56, No. 1, the initial figure is one measure long, beginning with the last (the unaccented) beat. At Ex. 57, No. 1, it is very brief,—one short measure, beginning with the accent. At Ex. 60, No. 1, it covers two measures, beginning with the second beat. At Ex. 57, No. 2, it is very long,—four measures, or an entire Phrase. At Ex. 55, No. 3, it begins upon the 6th beat of the 9-8 measure.

Illustrations of the rare recurrence of a group of *less or more* beats than the fundamental rhythmic group contains, are given in Ex. 62.

EXERCISES IN MELODY-WRITING.   43

63. The recurrences, by Repetition or Sequence, may take place at any point in the Phrase or Period; though they are most common at the beginning,—and, in any case, *must represent corresponding rhythmic pulses* (beats or measures), as indicated in the last clause of par. 56.

In Ex. 49, measure 3 is a sequence of measure 2 (three steps lower); and measures 5, 6 and 7 are the repetition of measures 1, 2 and 3, that constitute the "parallel construction" of the whole Period. In Ex. 50, measure 2 is a sequence of measure 1, and measure 7 a sequence of measure 6. In Ex. 53, No. 1, measure 6 is a repetition of measure 2.

64. Besides the obvious structural merit of such unified formations, there is another important and peculiar advantage involved, namely:

> The recurrence of a group of tones, by repetition or sequence, serves to rectify, or at least to justify, almost any irregularities of melodic succession which may occur,
>
> (1) *At the point of contact* of the symmetrical groups, or,
>
> (2) *During the sequential recurrence* of any perfectly faultless initial group.

This rule is analogous to that of par. 56, in reference to the amelioration of irregularities of rhythm,—by symmetrical recurrence. For illustration:

65. The manifest importance of brief rests, at the *end* of the symmetrical groups, to emphasize the effect of their recurrence, and exhibit the syntax of the Phrases, is demonstrated in Ex. 47, Nos. 1, 3, 4; Ex. 56, No. 2; Ex. 59, No. 3; Ex. 60, No. 3.

Review par. 49, and see also, Ex 49, No 1; Ex. 50; Ex 52, No. 4; Ex. 56, No. 2; Ex. 59, Nos. 3, 4; Ex. 60, No 3; Ex. 64, No. 3; Ex. 95, No. 3; Ex. 100, No. 1.

LESSON 11.

A large number of 4 and 8-measure melodies, with symmetrical repetitions and sequences of tone-groups, as explained above.

CHAPTER XI.

MELODIC SYNTAX, CONTINUED.

REPETITION AND SEQUENCE, MODIFIED.

66. The recurrences of tone-groups, both as repetition and as sequence, need not be thus exact, as shown in the preceding chapter, but may be *modified*, or varied, slightly (not to such an extent as to render their recognition difficult or uncertain), as follows:

(a) By adding one or more intermediate tones;—possibly, also, by omitting particles of the initial group;

(b) By altering one or another of the original intervals of melodic succession,—widening a step-wise progression to a narrow leap, or a narrow leap to a wider one, and vice versa. In this way the lines of the initial group are somewhat expanded or contracted, but, as a rule, without changing the original *direction* at any point. Thus:

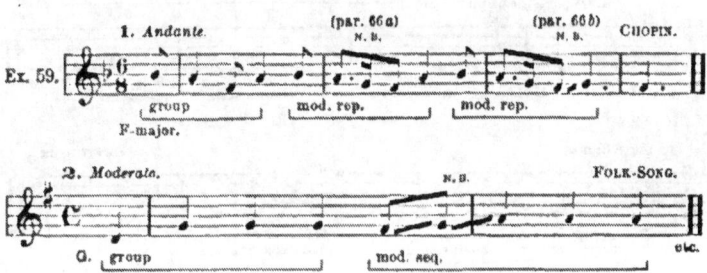

EXERCISES IN MELODY-WRITING. 45

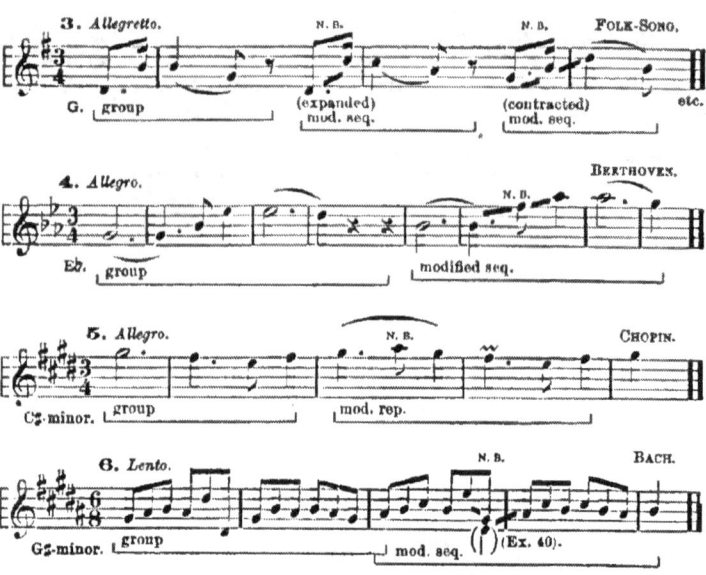

See also, Ex. 52, No. 3, measure 1 and 3; Ex. 52, No. 5, measures 1 and 5; Ex. 56, No. 1, compare last 4 tones with first 4.

67. Further, the repetition or sequence may be *partial;* that is, consisting in the recurrence of only a portion of the original group. For illustration:

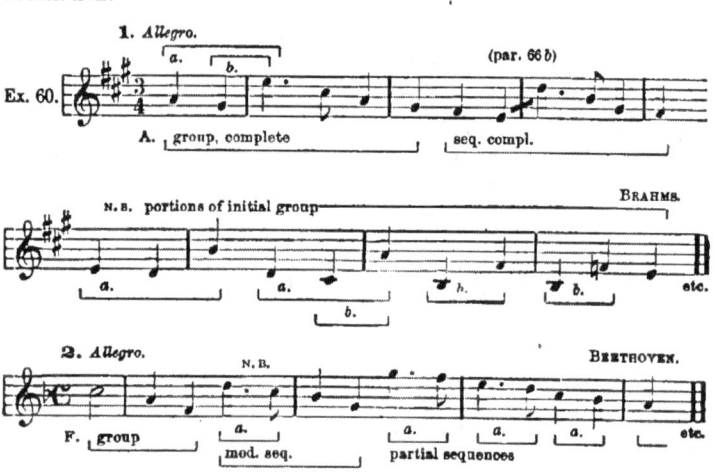

68. Further, more rarely, the repetition or sequence may appear in a *different rhythmic form.* This very effective mode of recurrence is comparatively harmless (not jeopardizing the recognizability of the original group):—

(1) If the *sum of beats remains the same;* or

(2) If the sum is exactly *divided,* or *doubled,* so that the prosodic arrangement (of accented and unaccented tones) is not altered. Thus:

69. Further, still more rarely, the recurrence by repetition or sequence may appear in a different *rhythmic location,* i. e., on other beats of the measure. This shifting of the measure, and consequent alteration of the original prosodic effect, is a very misleading device, and belongs, properly, only to the higher ranges of composition; for a time, yet, it should be avoided by the student, unless he can succeed in obviating total confusion of measure.

It may result:—

(1) From such *partial* recurrences as were shown in Ex. 60, No. 1; or

(2) From adopting a group which contains, originally, *less or more beats* than the number contained in a fundamental rhythmic group.

It is least objectionable when the irregular recurrence appears several times in succession,—until the original rhythmic location is regained. For illustration:

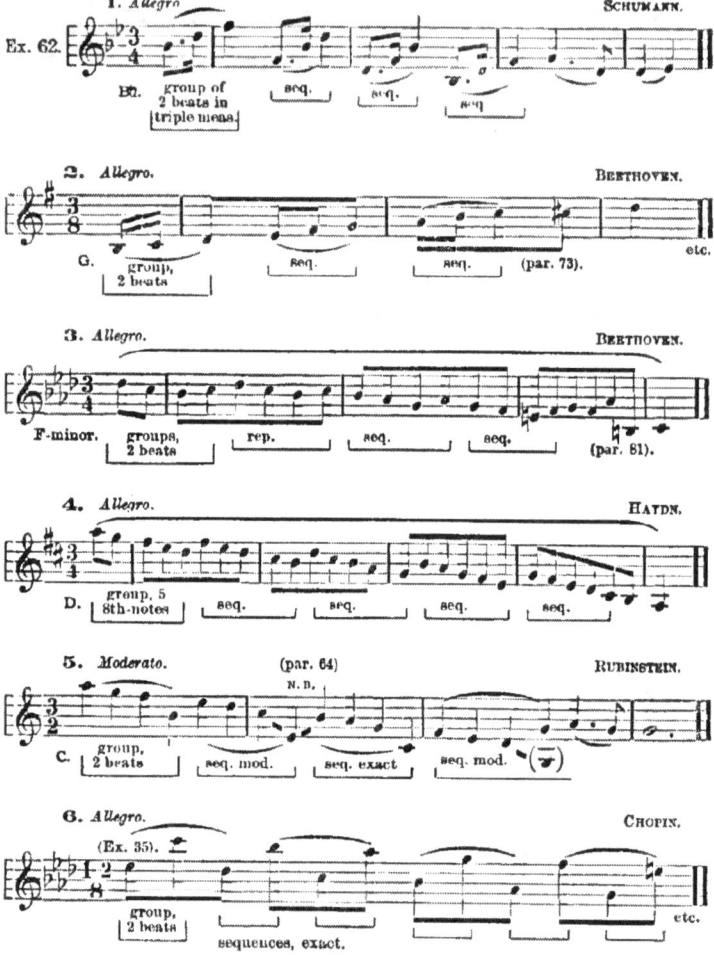

70. Finally, the recurrence may be modified by being turned *bodily* in the *contrary direction* (i. e., upside down). This is an excellent device and should be freely exercised. In this case, particularly, the recurrence should appear in corresponding rhythmic location (not shifted, as seen in Ex. 62, but according to the rule of par. 63); and, as a rule, should not be subjected to any *further* confusing modification that may obscure the syntactic purpose. Thus:

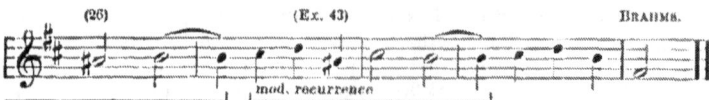

See also, Ex. 7, No. 4, first three tones, measures 1 and 3.

LESSON 12.

A large number of 4 and 8-measure melodies, with recurrences of tone-groups, by repetition or sequence, *modified* in the manners illustrated. Each device is to be exercised successively, in the order given above. Major and minor alternately; various species of Measure, from 2/4 to 12/8. No changes of key.

After correction, a few of these melodies may be harmonized.

CHAPTER XII.

MELODIC SYNTAX, CONTINUED.

THE PERIOD, RESUMED.

71. The recurrence by *Sequence* may be utilized on a broad scale, as a guide for the movements of the Consequent Phrase of a Period-form. In this case again, as in par. 52, the construction is "parallel," the only difference being, that "sequence" is substituted for "repetition," in the conduct of the second Phrase.

The sequential formation need not be exact; it is far more likely to be merely an *approximate* guide for the Consequent Phrase. And it need not, generally will not, extend through the *entire* Consequent, but through a portion only. Thus:

50   EXERCISES IN MELODY-WRITING.

See also, Ex. 57, No. 2; "TONE-RELATIONS," Lesson 48,—3.

N.B.—In Nos. 1 and 2 of the above example, the cadence-tones are not defined according to the rules of Chapters VII and IX; but the pupil can easily (and must, yet awhile) adjust his own exercises to those rules.

72. Analogously, the device of recurrence in *Contrary direction* (par. 70) may be applied on the same broad scale, to the construction of the Consequent Phrase;—possibly throughout the latter, though much more probably during a portion, only, of its length; and, almost certainly, with some freedom in regard to the modifications explained in par. 66.

Such melodies are known as Periods of "*opposite* construction"; compare pars. 52 and 53. For example:

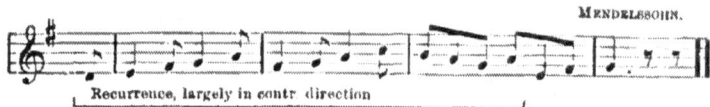

Recurrence, largely in contr direction

See also, "TONE-RELATIONS," Lesson 18, No. 7; 22, No. 3; 27, No. 1; 48, No. 6.

LESSON 13.

A large number of 8-measure melodies in Period-form, applying the devices of *sequence*, and of *contrary direction*, for such a portion of the Consequent Phrase as will not interfere with the given rules of the cadences.

The extent of coincidence (either as sequence, or in the opposite direction) is to be shortened, gradually, in the later exercises, similar to the manner dictated in par. 53,—until no more than brief figures (3 or 4 tones) of the Consequent are derived from the corresponding measures of the Antecedent;—not necessarily the *beginning*; the derivation may occur at *any point*.

Major and minor alternately.

All species of Measure, up to 9/8 or 9/4.

No changes of key.

Review, carefully, the directions given in Lesson 8, and apply them, where suitable.

CHAPTER XIII.

ALTERED SCALE-STEPS; MAJOR.

73. The Scale-line may be modified by the *chromatic Inflection* of certain steps; or by the *Substitution* of such chromatically inflected steps for the corresponding original ones.

N. B.—A chromatic progression is the inflection of a *letter*, by means of an Accidental.

The chromatic inflections are to be effectuated strictly in accordance with what are known as the "Altered Scale-steps."

These are as follows, in the *major mode* (arranged in the order of their frequency and excellence):

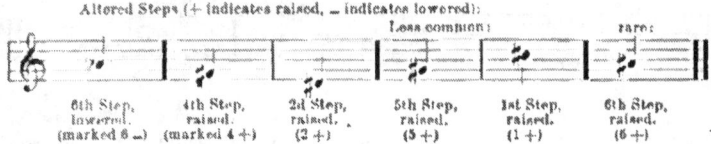

74. SUMMARY: Every Scale-step in major may be chromatically raised, i. e., inflected *upward*,—excepting the 3rd and 7th Steps (those which are followed, in ascending, by the half-steps). Only the 6th Scale-step, however, may be lowered, i. e., inflected *downward*.

75. Every altered Step in major may appear,

(*a*) Either as direct *chromatic inflection* of the original Step, that is, preceded by the latter; thus:

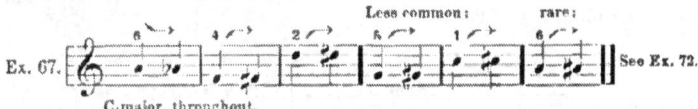

(*b*) Or, as *substitution* for the original Step. In this case, the altered Step may be approached from the neighboring Step,—best from that one which lies nearest the altered tone; and, as a rule, so as to avoid the interval of an augmented 2nd. Thus:

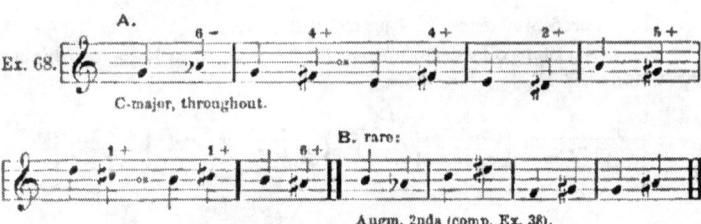

(*c*) Or the altered tone may be approached with a *leap*, exactly according to the rule of par. 28 *a*; i. e., with a skip from any not unreasonably distant tone *downward* to a *raised* Scale-step (because of its upward resolution,—par. 76 a); or from any tone *upward* to the *lowered* 6th Step (because of its downward resolution). Thus:

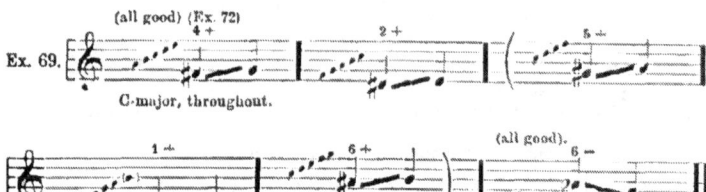

(d) Very rarely, the raised tones may be approached with the opposite leap, namely, from below,—in the direction corresponding to their resolution. For example:

(e) On the contrary, the lowered 6th Step (being a more natural inflection than any other of the altered tones) may easily be approached with an irregular skip, from above,—only, however, along some obvious chord-line in the prevailing key. Thus:

76. *(a)* The regular (to a certain extent obligatory) progression, or *Resolution* (par. 7), of the altered Scale-steps is as follows:

The lowered Step *descends,*—generally step-wise.

The raised Steps all *ascend,*—generally step-wise, i. e., to the *next* higher Scale-step. Thus:

(b) Exceptions: The lowered 6th Step, for the reason given in par. 75 *e*, may leap upward or downward, along any obvious chord-line. This is also possible with the *best* raised Steps (namely, the raised 4th and 2nd), but rare, and hazardous, because of the difficulty of confirming an *obvious*

chord-line, without cancelling the prevailing key; see par. 77. For illustration:

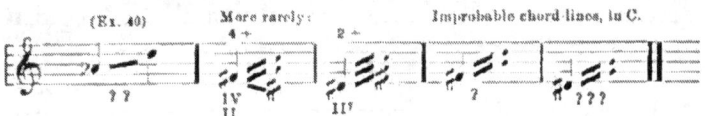

(c) Further, the *raised 4th and 2nd Steps* are, rarely, *pressed chromatically downward* to the original tones,—exactly according to the principle of par. 10, which review. Thus:

77. The inflected tones are not to be considered as *changes of the key*, nor allowed to cancel the prevailing scale. They are controlled in their movements by the impression of the given key (or scale), which is to remain the same throughout each Phrase or Period-melody,—for the present.

For general illustration:

See also, Ex. 64, No. 2 (c♯); and glance at par. 98.

LESSON 14.

A number of 4 and 8-measure melodies, in *Major*, with occasional inflected Steps. The alterations must not be so brief as to appear to be "grace-notes" only, but must be obviously *essential tones;* as a rule, not less than a full beat in length, occasionally longer. No changes of key are to take place (par. 77).

The first few exercises are to contain the *best* altered tones, and the *regular* modes of treatment; then experiments may be made with the more exceptional forms. Review par. 9 *a*; par. 30; par. 39.

CHAPTER XIV.

ALTERED SCALE-STEPS; MINOR.

78. The inflections of the *harmonic minor scale* are as follows (in the order of comparative importance):

These can not be as conveniently summarized as the altered Steps of major; they must be independently memorized.

79. The rules for their treatment are nearly, though not precisely, similar to those governing the altered Steps of major.

(a) The raised 4th Step (which appears alike in major and minor) is the only one that may occur both as chromatic inflection of, and as substitution for, the original Step; i. e., it may be introduced chromatically (par. 75 *a*), or from the nearest neighboring Step (par. 75 *b*), or with a skip from any *higher* tone (par. 75 *c*). Thus:

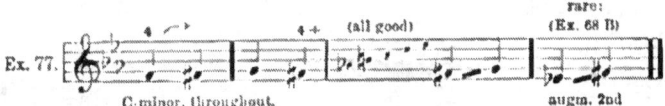

Ex. 77.

(b) The other altered tones, in minor, should not be introduced chromatically, but may appear only as *substitutions* for the corresponding Steps; best approached, as usual, from the nearest neighboring Step. The introduction with a leap is more rare,—excepting in the case of the raised 6th Step, which may be approached from any *higher* tone (par. 75 *c*); and the lowered 2nd Step, to which a skip may be made *from either side, along the line of an obvious chord*. Thus:

Ex. 78.

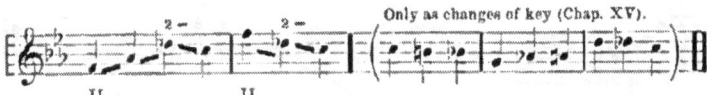

80. As in major (par. 76 *a*), the raised Steps are resolved upward, the lowered Steps downward,—generally to the adjacent Step. A few exceptions are possible, as seen in the following:

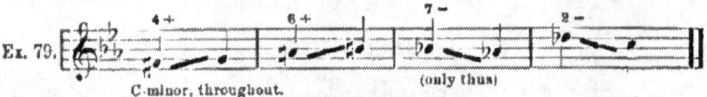

Ex. 79.

EXERCISES IN MELODY-WRITING. 57

For general illustration:

* This b-flat is a non-essential embellishing tone.

See also, Ex. 64, No. 2 (B♮ in 2nd measure, F♯ in 7th measure).

LESSON 15.

A number of 4 and 8-measure melodies, in *Minor*, with occasional inflected Steps. Review *par. 39*; par. 77; and *all the directions given in Lesson 14.*

CHAPTER XV.

MODULATION, OR CHANGES OF KEY.

81. A melody may be conducted away from the line of its own scale, into that of some other key. This effects a so-called Modulation.

The change of scale may be permanent, or it may be only temporary. In the first case, the melody, after passing over into the new key, makes its perfect cadence upon the Tonic of the latter. (See "Tone-Relations," all of Lessons 38 and 39.) When, on the other hand, the modulation is temporary (or transient, as it is called), the melody follows the line of the new scale only for a time (a few beats), and then returns to the original key. (See "Tone-Relations," all of Lesson 40.)

82. Rule I.—The original scale should be exchanged only for that of a *next-related key*. Of these there are five, namely: one with the *same* signature, two with the *next higher*, and two with the *next lower* signature (i. e. one sharp more or less, or one flat more or less). Thus:

From C-major (♮-signature), into
- a-minor (♮-signature).
- G-major (♯   "   ).
- e-minor (♯   "   ).
- F-major (♭   "   ).
- d-minor (♭   "   ).

Or: from f♯-minor (3♯-signature), into
- A-major (3♯-signature).
- E-major (4♯   "   ).
- c♯-minor (4♯   "   ).
- D-major (2♯   "   ).
- b-minor (2♯   "   ).

Or: from A♭-major (4♭-signature), into
- f-minor (4♭-signature).
- E♭-major (3♭   "   ).
- c-minor (3♭   "   ).
- D♭-major (5♭   "   ).
- b♭-minor (5♭   "   ).

N. B.—Capital letters indicate major keys; small letters, minors.

83. Rule II.—The change of key may be made at any point in the Phrase, upon either an accented or an unaccented beat. But it must,—at present,—take place *after one of the three tones which constitute the Tonic chord,*

i. e., either after the 1st, the 3rd, or the 5th Step of the momentary scale (namely, the *Inactive* steps, par. 5). Thus:

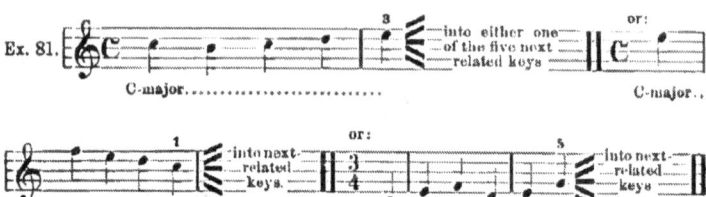

Ex. 81.

84. RULE III.—The deflection of the melody into the desired scale may,—after reaching one of the Inactive tones indicated in Rule II,—be effected by *passing through any one of the five tones which constitute the chord of the Dominant-9th,* i. e., either the 5th, 7th, 2nd, 4th, or 6th Scale-steps of the desired key;—in other words, an entrance may be effected into the desired key through *any other than its 1st and 3rd Scale-steps.* (Even these may be used, as will be seen in time; but not at present.)

The most powerful of these "modulatory tones" is the 7th Scale-step (the so-called Leading-tone); still, all five are equally adequate, if properly approached and properly treated.

85. *(a)* If possible, the *last tone of the first key* (one of the Inactive Steps given in Rule II) *should be transformed mentally into a Scale-step of the prospective key.* The melody then runs on, from the footing thus secured in the new scale, in exact accordance with former rules. For illustration:

Ex. 82 A.

(b) The most satisfactory result is gained (as far as the melody itself is concerned) by using, as soon as the new key is entered, a tone, or a group of tones, which indicates very distinctly the Dominant harmony of the key,—

so that the Leading-tone, or some other tone *that distinguishes the new key from the preceding one,* is instantly, or very soon, introduced. Ex. 82 A, No. 1, would be more *definite* thus:

86. If this mental transformation (par. 85 a) is not possible: that is, if the last tone of one scale *does not belong to the coming key,* then a *chromatic progression* will need to be made, at that point,—by simply inserting an accidental (see par. 73, N. B.). Thus:

87. *(a)* If such a chromatic movement be necessary, it should be foreseen, and properly *approached,* i. e., in the *corresponding direction.* Thus:

(b) Or, the chromatic progression may be prepared by a wide leap from the opposite side, involving a change of direction, according to par. 26. Thus:

(*c*) Or, finally, the chromatic inflection may be avoided, in the melody itself, by moving *step-wise* in the *opposite direction*. This involves the assumption of a Diminished-7th chord (i. e., the Incomplete Dominant-9th, in its minor form),—where the new key begins; and implies that the chromatic tone is taken up in some other part of the harmonic body. Thus:

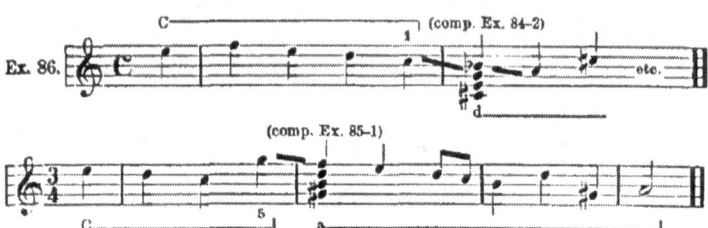

For general illustration (capitals, major; small letters, minor):

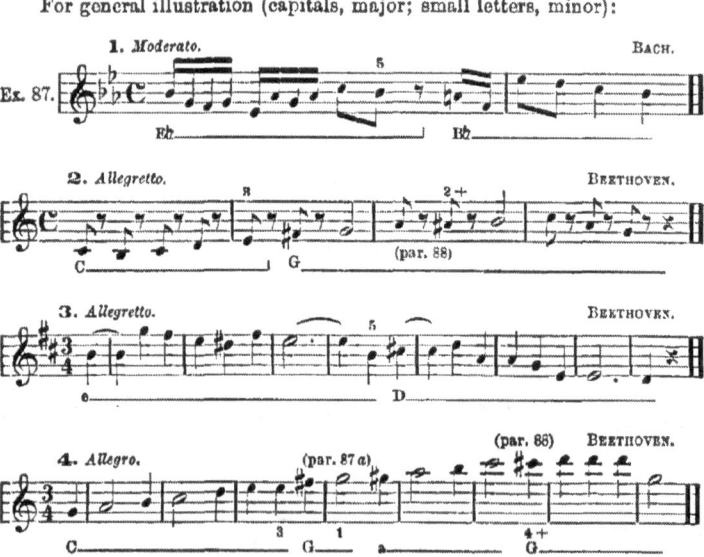

88. Whether the foreign tones in a melody are merely *inflected Scale-steps* (i. e. altered tones), or the indicators of *Modulation* (i. e., change of entire scale, into that of another key), depends

(1) Partly upon the location of the foreign tone in the prevailing key; for in order to serve as altered Step, it must conform to the lists given for major and minor in Exs. 66 and 76. But,

(2) It also depends, much more largely (very often entirely), upon the

option of the composer, who, in the majority of cases, may treat the foreign tone, *in his harmonization,* either as momentary inflection (without abandoning the key), or as a modulatory tone (passing on into the corresponding new scale).

LESSON 16.

A number of 4-measure melodies in Phrase-form, beginning alternately in major and minor, with one (permanent) modulation in each, into some next-related key, closing with the perfect cadence upon the Tonic of the new key. Ex. 86, No. 2, may serve as a general model. Every species of Measure, from 3/8 to 12/8; the rhythm freely diversified. An occasional altered Step may be introduced.

CHAPTER XVI.

MODULATION, CONTINUED.

89. The process of modulation is precisely the same for *transient* changes of key, as for the permanent ones illustrated in the preceding lesson.

(a) In phrases in the smaller varieties of Measure, only one transient modulation is feasible, as a rule; i. e., the melody passes soon into one of the five next-related keys, and, after a few beats, returns and closes upon the Tonic of the *original* key. Thus:

(b) In the larger species of Measure (6/8, 9/8, 12/8), two or more transient modulations may be made in one phrase; only, however, among the

EXERCISES IN MELODY-WRITING. 63

5 next-related keys of the original scale, and, in each case, returning to the latter and cadencing upon its Tonic, as usual. Thus:

LESSON 17.

A number of 4-measure melodies in Phrase-form:

A. In the smaller species of Measure, with one transient modulation, and return (par. 89 *a*).

B. In larger Measures, with two or more transient modulations, and return (par. 89 *b*).

CHAPTER XVII.

MODULATION, PERIOD-FORMS.

90. Changes of key may occur in the Period-form, at any point in either Phrase; but they are likely to have especial bearing upon the semi-cadence, which may be made upon either one of the *three tones of the Tonic Triad* (Steps 1, 3 or 5) of a next-related key.

The best and most common keys selected for the semicadence are,

The Dominant key (one sharp more, or one flat less, than the original signature); and

The Relative key (the same signature).

The Dominant key is particularly appropriate for the semicadence of a Period beginning in major; the Relative key for one beginning in minor;

though both are possible for either mode,—and other next-related keys also. The most unusual is a semicadence in the Subdominant key (one flat more, or one sharp less, than the original signature). For illustration:

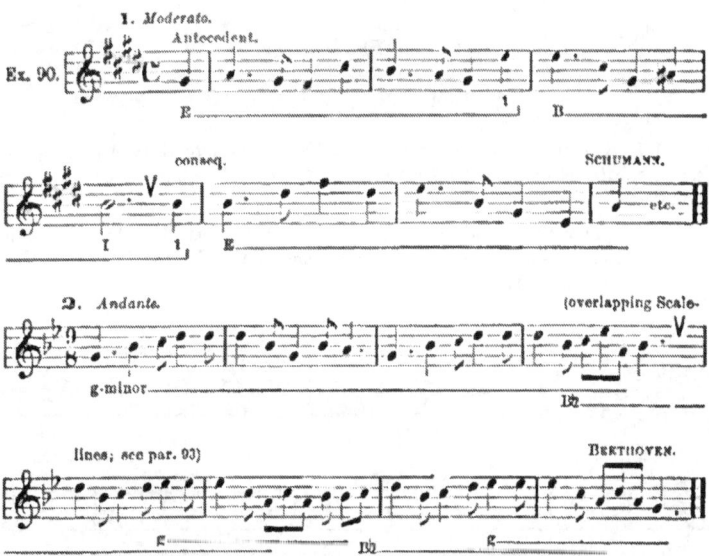

During the Consequent Phrase any transient modulations may be made, but the final cadence must fall upon the Tonic of the original key.

LESSON 18.

A number of 8-measure melodies in Period-form, according to the directions given in Chapters VII and IX, containing modulations (and occasional altered Steps) as explained above. Every species of Measure; major and minor beginning, alternately.

CHAPTER XVIII.

MODULATION, CHROMATIC.

91. The change of key may be effected contrary to Rule II (par. 83),—namely, after *other* than the Inactive 1st, 3rd or 5th Steps of the key,—on condition

That the melody progress *chromatically*, from the Step chosen to close the first key, into a proper tone of the desired key (Rule III, par. 84). Thus:

LESSON 19.

A number of 4 and 8-measure melodies, illustrating this device of chromatic modulation. Begin in major and minor alternately; all species of Measure (2/4 up to 12/8).

CHAPTER XIX.
OVERLAPPING SCALE-LINES.

92. General exceptions to the three rules of modulation given in Chapter XV (especially II and III) may be justified by mentally transforming a certain tone or tones of one key (no matter which scale-steps they represent) into some plausible Step or Steps,—if possible into more urgent and suggestive ones,—of the desired next-related key, and then continuing along the new line, without the formal observance of strict rules of modulation. This may even apply to some *more distant* key, if melodic conditions are favorable.

93. Such overlapping of scales,—a very common, but more difficult and exceptional method of modulation,—represents the application of par. 85 *a* in a broader sense, and is based upon the general principle that *a change of key may always be effected at (or through) any tone that is common to both keys concerned;*—especially when *two or more* such common tones appear in succession, so that the lines of the keys overlap for a number of beats (see Ex. 90, No. 2, which illustrates the point very strikingly);—or where there is a *pause in the melodic movement* (a tone of comparatively long duration), which affords time to apprehend the transformation (Ex. 92, Nos. 3 and 5; Ex. 91, No. 5).

This, it is true, will usually result as a matter of course from the application of the strict rules given in Chapter XV; but it has a much wider operation, and extends to many cases not included in these rules. For illustration:

EXERCISES IN MELODY-WRITING. 67

94. This agreement of key-lines is frequently turned to account in *substituting the opposite mode* (i. e., major for minor, or minor for major) of the key toward which the modulation was obviously directed according to the rule of next-relationship. This is usually an easy exchange, because the lines of the *corresponding* major and minor keys (i. e., corresponding in *key-note*) are so nearly coincident. See Ex. 37. For illustration:

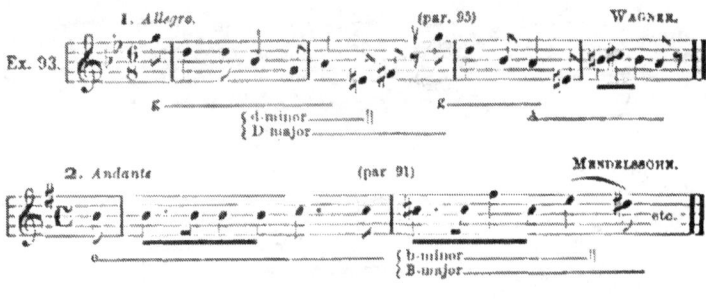

LESSON 20.

A number of 4 and 8-measure melodies, with modulations through common tones (by overlapping scales), as explained above. At first into *next-related* keys only. Then experiments may also be made with more remote keys. The general harmonic (chord) basis must be kept well in mind.

CHAPTER XX.

MODULATION IN SEQUENCES, AND AT CADENCES.

95. The broadest range of exceptional modulations is that afforded

(1) By *sequential recurrences* (par. 64); and

(2) By taking advantage of any sufficiently *well-defined pause*, or break (or cadence), in the line of the melody. Sequential recurrences generally involve, of themselves, such "breaks" in the melodic line,—at the points of contact. The "breaks," or cadences, may, however, be created by many other means. For example:

EXERCISES IN MELODY-WRITING. 69

See also, Ex. 91, No. 4; Ex. 92, Nos. 3 and 4; Ex. 95, Nos. 4 and 5.

LESSON 21.

A number of 4 and 8-measure melodies, with modulations in sequences, and at cadences or interruptions, as shown above. The transitions may be made either into next-related or remote keys, at option; and the melodies may close in any key,—best, however, upon the original Tonic. All species of measure. The sequences, and all breaks in the line of the melody, must be distinctly defined.

A few melodies may finally be made, extending beyond the regular 4 or 8-measure dimension (5, 6,—9, 10, 12 measures in length).

CHAPTER XXI.

CHROMATIC MELODY.

96. The principle of *chromatic succession* enunciated in par. 91 may be extended to a longer series of chromatic tones,—generally in similar direction. Such chromatic lines may represent a succession of brief and abrupt changes of key; or, as is far more likely, they may embody simply the principle of *altered Steps* (Chapters XIII and XIV).

EXERCISES IN MELODY-WRITING. 71

In the latter case, though they assert themselves (by their time-values) as essential tones, they prove to be, in reality, no more than intermediate tones, inserted between the tones of certain chord-lines in such a manner as not to overpower the impression of the prevailing key. For illustration:

LESSON 22.

A number of melodies, 4, 8 or 12 measures, with occasional continuous chromatic successions. The chromatic tones must be obviously essential, each not less than a full beat in value; and, as a rule, the succession should not extend beyond 5 or 6 tones.

CHAPTER XXII.

THE DOUBLE-PERIOD.

97. The Double-period generally embraces 16 measures; that is, four Phrases of four measures each, closing respectively with cadences in the 4th, 8th, 12th and 16th measures. Compare par. 50.

98. *(a)* The *first* of these is a light semicadence, and may be made upon any Step of the original key, as no modulation is likely to occur during the first Phrase of this longer design.

(b) The *second* one is apt to be a perfect cadence, falling upon the *Tonic* note of some next-related key,—best, as indicated in par. 90, the Dominant key (most commonly in a major melody), or the Relative key (usually in a minor melody); or perhaps the Relative of the Dominant; *very rarely*, either the Sub-dominant or its Relative.

(c) The *third* one is again a light semicadence, and may fall upon any tone of the Tonic Triad (Steps 1, 3 or 5) of that next-related key into which the melody may have been conducted; for, during the third Phrase, modulations may be freely made among any of the *next-related* keys,—rarely to remote keys. The best keys for this cadence are, either the Sub-dominant or its Relative.

(d) The *fourth* Phrase may also modulate freely, for a measure or two, but must then turn back definitely into the original scale, and must close, naturally, with the regular perfect cadence, upon the original key-note.

99. *(a)* The designs given in Chapter VII, in reference to parallel and contrasting construction (par. 52 and 53), must be closely followed in the *second half* of the Double-period (i. e., Phrases 3 and 4): at first, the *whole of Phrase 3* must correspond (perhaps with a few slight changes) to *Phrase 1;* and the greater part of *Phrase 4* must pursue the line of *Phrase 2*,—until the necessary difference of cadence asserts itself.

(b) Then, in each succeeding example, the parallelism is to be diminished gradually until, ultimately, the second pair of Phrases differs entirely

EXERCISES IN MELODY-WRITING. 73

from the melody of the first pair (totally contrasting construction). For illustration:

LESSON 23.

A number of 16-measure Double-periods, according to the above directions. Beginning in major and minor alternately; modulating at option; the principal species of Measure (3/4, 4/4, 6/8, 3/8, 6/4, 3/2, 9/8).

The harmonization of these melodies, after correction and approval by the teacher, may be undertaken by pupils familiar with the process.

DIVISION TWO.

UNESSENTIAL, OR EMBELLISHING, TONES.

CHAPTER XXIII.

DISTINCTION BETWEEN ESSENTIAL AND UNESSENTIAL TONES.

100. Not all the tones in a melody need be *essential*, i e , calling for special consideration in the process of harmonization. Many tones may be, and generally are, no more than *unessential adjuncts* of the principal (i. e., the essential or important) tones, which latter they merely serve either to connect or to embelish.

<small>Such embellishing tones have appeared in many of the foregoing illustrations, simply because their employment in composition is so common that but very few examples could be found in which they are absent.</small>

The distinction between Essential and Unessential tones is determined very largely by their *length;* usually, a tone of the value of a full beat is a principal or essential one; and, of two, three, or four quick tones that constitute the subdivisions of a beat, one or more are almost certain to be unessential.

But this is only the *general* distinction,—the true one depending, after all, upon the relation of the tones, whether short or long, to the *prevailing chord-line.* For illustration

This being the case, it follows, here again, that a melody must be designed with strict regard to some harmonic basis, or subconscious *chord-concept* (Review pars. 15, 23, 38,) The tones which agree with the momentary chord are the essential or harmonic tones; those which differ from it

are unessential embellishing, or inharmonic tones. Thus devised, or thus articulated, a melody is easy to harmonize.

THE SUSPENSION.

101. RULE I.—Any tone *which progresses step-wise* (along the scale-line, or chromatically) may be tied to the following, next lower or higher, tone, and thus be held over during a fraction of the value of the latter, as embellishment by *Suspension*. Thus:

This device is as simple as it is effective; and its result is invariably good, unless it be applied during some *very irregular* melodic progression, which the Suspension would probably aggravate.

102. *(a)* As a rule, the Suspension may best be introduced in *descending* step-wise progressions; but it is also good in ascending step-wise successions, especially when applied to tones which have a natural upward tendency, like the 7th scale-step (Leading-tone), or raised Steps.

(b) The obligatory movement of the Suspension forward into the essential tone, is its Resolution (par. 7).

(c) If irregularities of rhythm result, they may be redeemed by *recurrence*, precisely as shown in par. 56 a; see Ex. 100, Nos. 2 and 7.

(d) Instead of using a tie, the tone may be struck again, as repetition:

And in fact, in this form it may signify no more than simple tone-repetition, as indicated in par. 9 *a*, and practiced freely in all the preceding lessons.

(*e*) When applied to *single* tones in a measure or group, the best general effect is obtained at *accented* beats (as in Ex. 98, Nos. 2, 6 and 9, and in the majority of the following illustrations). But it is possible at the beginning of *any beat*, especially when occurring repeatedly, either in immediate succession (Ex. 99), or as recurrence at corresponding points (see par. 102 *c*).

(*f*) If the tie, or reiteration, is applied at a *skip* in the melody, the result will not be an inharmonic Suspension; but it will be correct if the tones represent some good chord-line. For general illustration:

"Tone-Relations," Lessons 57 and 58.

LESSON 24.

A. Take a number of former 4 or 8-measure melodies, and embellish them with occasional Suspensions, where convenient and effective, according to the above directions and illustrations.

B. Invent a number of 4 and 8-measure melodies (major and minor alternately) with special application of the Suspension. Use all species of Measure, and modulate at option. The pupil must not only hear each tone distinctly as he writes it, but must endeavor to realize the *chord-basis* also (i. e., the harmonic accompaniment).

EXERCISES IN MELODY-WRITING.

CHAPTER XXIV.

THE ANTICIPATION.

103. RULE II.—Any essential tone in the original (simple) melodic concept, or any weighty tone, whether essential or not, may be *anticipated* upon a fraction of the preceding beat,—usually a *very brief* fraction. Thus:

N. B.—This embellishment involves tone-repetition from one beat into the next, as in the Suspension, and is often not distinguishable from the latter at all. The difference lies solely in the purpose, or conception, of the writer, but may manifest itself clearly through the *following conditions:*

(1) The Anticipation is generally a very *short* tone;

(2) It is not *tied* to the following repetition, but is re-struck;

(3) If embellishment by Anticipation, the *second* of the two similar tones will be the essential one, and may progress in any manner; if embellishment by Suspension, the second tone will prove to be the unessential one, and must progress step-wise. This, again, depends upon the chord-basis.

See also Ex. 59, No. 3; and "TONE-RELATIONS," Lesson 60.

LESSON 25.

A. A number of former, simple, melodies, to be embellished with occasional Anticipations.

B. New melodies, with Anticipations,—and an occasional Suspension.

CHAPTER XXV.

THE PASSING-NOTE.

104. RULE III.—Any *skip of a third* between two successive essential (or weighty) tones in a melody, may be filled out, or reduced to step-wise progression, by *inserting the intermediate scale-step as Passing-note*. Usually the Passing-note takes exactly half the value of the first tone, but it may be *less* than this (rarely more) according to the desired rhythmic effect. See also par. 102 c. For illustration:

106. The Passing-note generally occurs, as seen in the above illustrations, upon an *unaccented* fraction of the beat,—within the beat or group represented by the first tone, and, consequently, without displacing the second tone of the original skip. But it is also possible to defer the Passing-note (i. e., to shift it forward) so that it encroaches upon the beat of the second tone, thus assuming the *accented* location, and dividing the value, of the latter. The rhythmic result is often much improved by this means. For example:

LESSON 26.

A. A number of former melodies, to be embellished with *occasional* Passing-notes, where skips of a 3rd occur.

B. New melodies, 4 and 8 measures, major and minor alternately, in various species of Measure,—with *occasional* Passing-notes, as shown above. Suspensions, Anticipations, and other material of past lessons must not be neglected.

CHAPTER XXVI.

PASSING-NOTES, CONTINUED.

106. A skip of a *fourth* may be filled out, similarly, by inserting the two intermediate scale-steps successively, in the *same direction*.

The two connected passing-notes may be both unaccented (i. e., located within the beat or rhythmic group of the first tone), or they may be disposed in any other manner between the two essential tones, according to the desired rhythmic effect. Compare par. 105, and par. 102 c. For illustration:

See also, Ex. 36, No. 17, first measure.

107. Adjacent scale-steps may be connected by the intermediate *chromatic* tone (where the space is a whole step). Such chromatic passing-notes actually corroborate, in origin and purpose, the Altered scale-steps (Chapters XIII and XIV), and are therefore more common in *ascending*, than in descending, succession. They differ in effect from the Altered Steps, which are essential tones, in being more *transient*, and therefore obviously *unessential*.

For larger spaces, alternate diatonic and chromatic passing-notes may be used in immediate succession in the same direction. For example:

See also Ex. 75, No. 7, measure 1.

108. As the fourth is the widest interval that can occur between contiguous chord-tones (namely, from the chord-fifth to the Root above), it follows that a line of intermediate passing-notes, inserted between still larger skips (5th, 6th, 7th or 8ve), can not consist exclusively of inharmonic tones, but must contain one or more chord-tones, also. The effect of the whole conjunct group, however, will be that of *unessential* tones, especially in swift successions; and as such they are to be regarded and treated. For illustration (the "harmonic" passing-notes indicated by × in parenthesis):

109. The device of tone-repetition, employed throughout the foregoing lessons, may be applied even to passing-notes. Such *repeated passing-notes* are best when they are of sufficient time-value, and importance, to be partly "essential" in effect. Thus:

EXERCISES IN MELODY-WRITING.   87

LESSON 27.

A. Former melodies, to be embellished with *occasional* passing-notes (diatonic, chromatic, and repeated), at skips of any size, but with strict regard to a sensible rhythmic result.

B. New melodies, with direct application of these passing-notes. The material of former lessons must be remembered, and employed.

CHAPTER XXVII.

NEIGHBORING-NOTES.

110. *(a)* RULE IV.—Any essential tone in a simple melodic line, or a weighty tone whether essential (harmonic) or not, may be embellished by placing either *its higher or its lower Neighbor before it.*

(b) Very frequently the essential tone *precedes*, as well as follows, the neighboring-tone, thus constituting an embellishing group of *three tones* (i. e., the essential or principal tone and its recurrence, with the upper or lower neighbor between;—or, in other words, the neighbor inserted between an ordinary tone-repetition).

(c) The group may assume almost any rhythmic form; either of the three tones may occupy the accented fraction of a beat, and the values are optional. But the simplest, and by far the most common form, is that

in which all three tones belong to the same beat, or rhythmic **group**. Thus:

111. The difference between the Neighboring-note and the Passing-note is, that the former *turns back into its own* principal tone, while the latter *passes on into another* essential tone. Compare Ex. 103, No. 1, with Ex. 108, carefully. In other words, the embellishment with a neighboring-note involves only *one* essential or weighty tone; the passing-note, on the contrary, always involves *two different* essential tones. The former is therefore a *local* embellishment, the latter a *progressive* one.

112. Whether the upper or the lower neighbor is to be used, depends somewhat upon *the location of the following tone* in the original melodic line. The rules are:

(1) If the formation of the group is to be *Regular*, the upper neighbor is taken when the next tone lies below; and, vice versa, the lower neighbor when the following tone lies higher;—or, in other words, that neighbor is chosen which lies *opposite* the coming tone. In this way, the impetus imparted to the final tone in the group by its embellishing neighbor, **carries** it naturally *toward* the next tone. Thus:

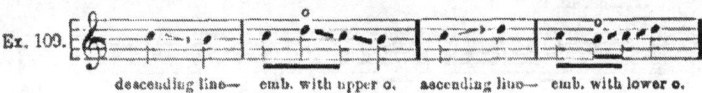

Or (2), in a *series* of such groups, each may be turned the *same way,* irrespective of the direction into the next essential tone. In this case, some of the groups will be *Irregular*,—but their irregularity is counteracted, as usual, by "uniform recurrence" (par. 56 a). For example:

N. B.—In any case, the *rhythmic* arrangement of such successive (or corresponding) groups is almost certain to be uniform.

113. Further, the *notation* of the neighboring-notes is subject to the following rules:

(1) The *upper* neighbor must always agree with the line of the prevailing scale. Thus:

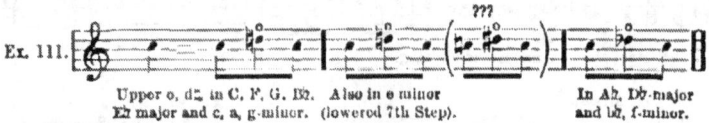

(2) The *lower* neighbor may also agree in notation with the line of the prevailing scale, and in melodies of a serious or stately character (or when the neighboring note is long) it does so. But ordinarily, especially in graceful or rapid melodies, the *lower neighbor lies a half-step below its principal tone*, irrespective of key;—excepting when the principal tone is the 7th

scale-step (the Leading-tone), for which the lower *whole step* is almost always chosen. Thus:

LESSON 28.

A. A number of simple melodies in *uniform rhythm* (from the first five lessons), to be embellished with 3-tone groups, as shown above.

They may be applied to an occasional single tone, in which case the rhythmic effect must be guarded; if *unaccented* beats are broken, the rhythm will be regular; if irregular, from any cause, the rhythm must be rectified by "recurrence."

Or the groups may appear continuously, i. e., at each tone throughout the melody, generally excepting the final (cadence) tone; this will constitute a "Running part."

B. New melodies, 4 and 8 measures, in various species of Measure, major and minor alternately, with special reference to the 3-tone group. The material of former lessons must not be neglected.

CHAPTER XXVIII.

NEIGHBORING-NOTES, CONTINUED.

114. These, in a sense fundamental, embellishing groups of three tones, may be enlarged to four, five, six, or more tones in many ways:

(1) By adding to the 3-tone group (either before or after) any tone which belongs to the *chord-line* of the essential tone. Thus:

(2) By adding a *passing-note* (before or after).

N.B.—Review par. 111, in reference to the distinction between neighboring and passing-notes. And bear in mind, while studying these somewhat confusing forms, that every neighboring-note must be *preceded*, as well as followed, by its principal tone (par. 110 b).

For illustration.

(3) By inserting first one and then *the other* neighboring-note between reiterations of their principal tone.

This will result, at first, in groups of at least *five* tones—which may then be enlarged, precisely as shown above. Thus:

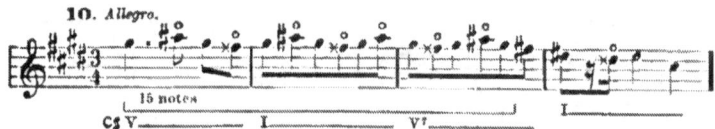

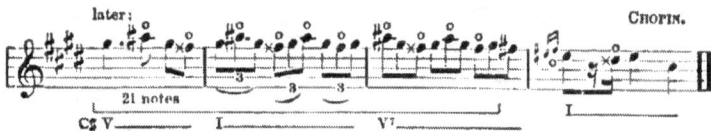

(4) More rarely, by repetition of the neighboring-note (similar to par. 109). Thus:

Ex. 116.

LESSON 29.

A. A few former melodies in uniform rhythm, to be embellished with these larger groups,—either at occasional single points, or throughout, as indicated in the preceding lesson.

B. New melodies, with especial reference to these forms of embellishment.

CHAPTER XXIX.

NEIGHBORING-NOTE AS APPOGGIATURA.

115. The neighboring-note, instead of appearing thus *between reiterations* of its principal tone, may, moreover, be placed *simply before* the latter,—*preceding* it only, as prefixed grace-note, and forming an embellishing group of but *two* tones (compare par. 110 *a* and *b*). In this connection it is called an *Appoggiatura.* Its details are subject to the rules given in Chapter XXVII.

(1) The rhythmic form, and the location, of the 2-tone group are optional; but the appoggiatura is most commonly placed upon the *accented* fraction of the beat (like the suspension, or the accented passing-note, and, like these, changing the original location of the essential tone by shifting it forward); and the appoggiatura is quite frequently longer than its principal tone. For example:

EXERCISES IN MELODY-WRITING. 97

(2) The choice between upper or lower neighboring-note, as appoggiatura, may be determined, primarily, by the rules given above;—i. e., either according to the *direction* into the following essential tone (see Ex. 117, Nos. 6, 7, 9 and 11); or in *uniform* figures, as in Ex. 117, Nos. 2 and 8. But, in practical composition, the utmost freedom is exercised in this choice. In general, the upper neighbor is the more common. The greatest influence is apparently exerted by the location of the *preceding* tone; for instance:

An *upward* movement (especially with a skip) is usually made to the *upper* appoggiatura; and a *downward* progression to the *lower* one,—of the following tone, of course. This simply corroborates the rule given in par. 28 a, and again in par. 75 c; i. e., the appoggiatura is best approached (from *any* distance) in the direction *opposite to that of its Resolution* (its obligatory step-wise progression into its principal tone). For illustration:

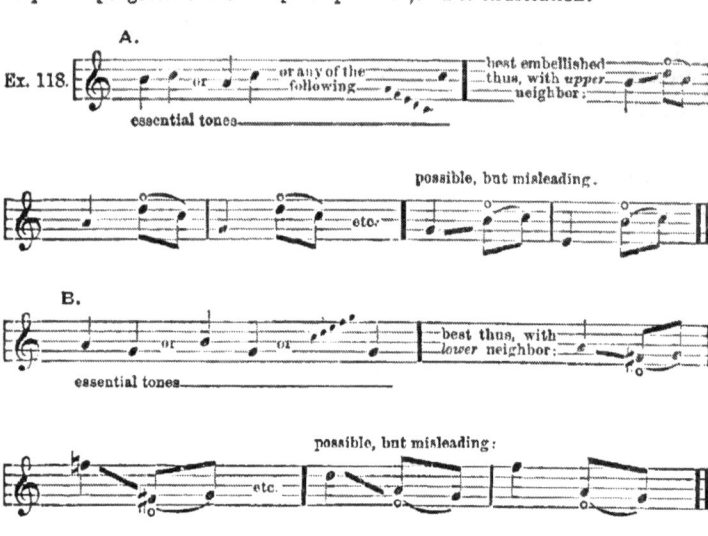

This rule prevails almost throughout Ex. 117; the only exceptions occur in No. 5 (second measure), and in No. 8 (second half of each measure).

(3) The notation of the appoggiatura is defined *exactly* according to the rules given in par. 113 (Exs. 111 and 112).

(4) The presence of an appoggiatura justifies exceptions to the rule of successive skips in the same direction, given in par. 31 (Ex. 25, Nos. 6, 11, 12, 13, 14). For example:

See also Ex. 121, No. 5.

LESSON 30.

A. A number of former melodies, to be embellished with the **appoggiatura**, in 2-tone groups; either at single points, or at each tone throughout (in melodies of uniform rhythm).

B. New melodies, 4 and 8 measures, major and minor alternately, in various species of Measure,—with especial reference to this form of embellishment. Former devices must be borne in mind and employed.

CHAPTER XXX.

DOUBLE-APPOGGIATURA.

116. *(a)* In a similar manner, and with similar, though much heightened, effect, *both* the upper and lower neighbor may *successively* precede their mutual principal tone, as *Double-appoggiatura*. The first appoggiatura does not progress directly into its principal tone, but passes first over to the opposite neighbor (of the *same* principal tone), thus producing a new variety of the 3-tone group. Compare Ex. 108; and observe the distinction between this use of both neighbors, and that illustrated in Ex. 115.

For example:

essential tone   emb. with Double-appogg.

(b) As usual, the group may appear in any reasonable rhythmic form; either of the 3 tones may occupy the accented fraction of the beat or rhythmic group; and the time-values are almost wholly optional. The details of treatment conform to the rules and illustrations of the preceding chapter. For example:

EXERCISES IN MELODY-WRITING.

117. Very frequently the Double-appoggiatura is *preceded*, as well as followed, by the principal tone, thus extending the figures shown in Exs. 121 and 108 to a new species of *four-tone* group, which is one of the most convenient, effective and common forms in the entire range of melodic embellishment. The reiteration of the principal tone is separated by *both* the upper and lower neighbor *in succession*,—in either order, and in any rational rhythmic form. Thus:

118. In rare instances, the number of these interposed neighboring-notes is increased to *three*, by returning to the first appoggiatura before passing on into the essential tone. Thus:

EXERCISES IN MELODY-WRITING. 105

LESSON 31.

A. A number of former melodies, to be embellished with the Double appoggiatura, in the 3-tone and 4-tone groups above illustrated; either occasionally, or continuously.

B. New melodies, 4 and 8 measures, major and minor, in various species of Measure, with special reference to this form of embellishment.

CHAPTER XXXI.

APPOGGIATURAS, CONTINUED.

119. The Double-appoggiatura sometimes appears in connection with the Suspension, as "indirect Resolution" of the latter. The Suspension, as is made manifest in Chapter XXIII, is *always* a neighbor of the following essential tone,—because of its invariable application at a *step-wise* progression,—either above or below. Hence, it may be regarded as an appoggiatura, and be conducted first into the *opposite* neighbor, before the essential tone follows, precisely as shown in par. 116 a. For example:

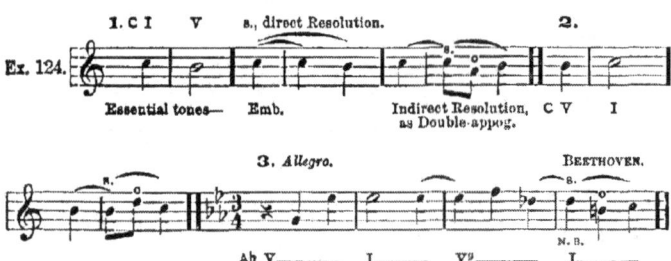

120. The strict rule of the neighboring-note, as seen throughout the preceding chapters, is, that it must be *followed by a step-wise Resolution* into its principal tone,—either immediately, or after swinging over into the opposite neighbor of that principal tone.

(*a*) A peculiar, but quite common, exception to this rule is, that the *upper* neighboring-note, after properly following its principal tone, may *leap down a 3rd.* In other words,—the *upper* neighbor may intervene between two principal tones that represent a *descending step-wise* progression. The result is best when the principal tones are both harmonic; but it is applicable to any weighty tones, even when one, or each of them, is a passing-note.

This,—the "Unresolved,"—neighboring-note is *always unaccented*, and usually *short* (like the anticipation, which it most resembles in origin and character). Thus:

EXERCISES IN MELODY-WRITING.   107

(b) If a modulation is made during a step-wise descending melodic passage which is to be embellished with the unresolved neighbor, the latter must agree in notation with the scale of the *following* principal tone,—of which, as above stated, it is properly speaking an anticipation. Thus:

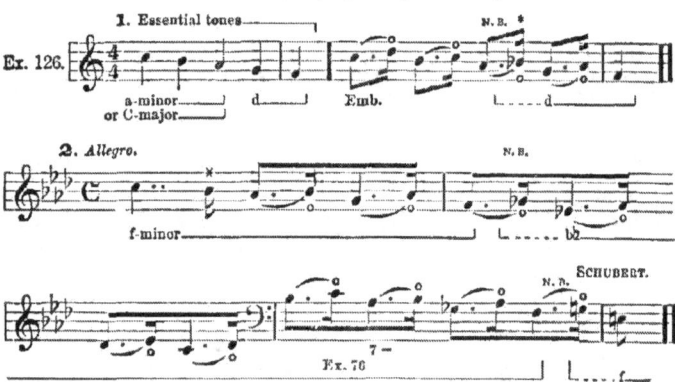

* Not b♮, unless the key remains C or a throughout.

(c) Much more rarely, this device is reversed; i. e., the *lower* neighbor is inserted between step-wise *ascending* tones. The rules correspond to the preceding. Thus:

(d) When the rhythm is uniform, and the *tempo* rapid, as in some of the above illustrations, these unresolved neighbors may often (not always) be analyzed as a Double-appoggiatura. Thus:

LESSON 32.

A. A number of former simple melodies (including those of Lesson 24), to be embellished with Suspensions with indirect Resolution; and with unresolved neighboring-notes, as shown above.

B. New melodies, with special reference to these embellishments.

CHAPTER XXXII.

EVOLUTION OF MELODIC GERMS.

121. The application of these various classes of embellishments is apt, in many cases, to be determined upon some broader basis than the general purpose of ornamenting individual tones of a simple melodic line.

The development or evolution of an elaborate melodic figure, or complete Phrase, out of two or three fundamental tones, by miscellaneous methods of embellishment and repetition, has been repeatedly exhibited in the foregoing examples; and while such products are not, as a rule, in *advanced* musical thought, the result of deliberate intention, they are none the less surely thus simple in their original germinal form, *and must have existed in this simple form* in the firmly established melodic habits of the composer,—even when they appear to have issued spontaneously from his mind, directly, in their complete ornate and characteristic shape.

This process of melodic evolution is so natural and so wholesome, and the evidences of its presence in classic melodic thought are so clear, so positive and so instructive, that its systematic exercise is of vital importance to the student who aims to acquire habits of healthy and facile melodic conduct.

The only rules are: that the fundamental tones (the germ) shall form a *perfectly faultless and natural* melodic figure, at least free from extreme irregularities; and that the manipulation of it into an ornate Phrase shall be coherent, smooth, well-balanced (as concerns the rhythmic and syntactic exterior), and free from eccentricity.

122. Hence, an ornate melodic sentence may conceal (perhaps so cleverly that its presence may scarcely be heard,—though it is certain to be *felt*) a part of the line of the scale; or the simplest elements of the Tonic chord, or Dominant chords.

The following illustrations are to be very studiously examined *and analyzed:*

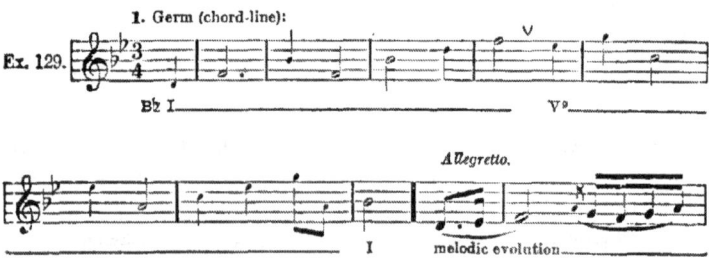

EXERCISES IN MELODY-WRITING. 111

EXERCISES IN MELODY-WRITING.

EXERCISES IN MELODY-WRITING. 113

123. Such simple germs, derived directly from the *scale*, or from some primary *chord-line*, are,—like the soil,—common property, open to the use of all humanity.

In the *choice* of these germs no originality can be exercised, or proven,—merely common sense.

But their *manipulation*,—the method, and the extent, of their embellishment and development,—exhibits the *individuality of the composer*, the particular quality and calibre of his innate musical susceptibility, or the degree of discrimination and "taste" that he has acquired by persistent and thorough exercise of such established technical methods as those expounded in the present treatise,—that may possibly lead onward into yet undiscovered modes of treatment.

This is one of the most obvious and natural phases of the apparently occult, but in reality very manifest, Science of Originality.

LESSON 33.

The evolution of complete, ornate and characteristic, melodic sentences, 4, 8, 12 or 16 measures in length (major and minor alternately, and in all species of Measure), out of simple germs, imitating the melodic and rhythmic methods shown in the above example.

CHAPTER XXXIII.

MELODIC EVOLUTION, CONTINUED.

124. Further, the application of these embellishing processes may serve to disguise, or to heighten the effect of, Repetitions, Sequences, and Recurrences of former figures or phrases in general. Review the text of Chapters X and XI; see Ex. 100, No. 3; Ex. 106, No. 4; Ex. 115, No. 10; and examine and *analyze* the following, thoroughly:

116 EXERCISES IN MELODY-WRITING.

EXERCISES IN MELODY-WRITING. 119

* These tones represent a "passing-group" (109, extended), in sequential formation.

120 EXERCISES IN MELODY-WRITING.

** This last illustration comes under the head of "manipulation" in general; it is based more upon *rhythmic* modification than melodic embellishment.

LESSON 34.

A. Former, or new, 4 and 8-measure melodies, with embellished *repetition*.

B. Melodies, of optional length, with special application of the modified (embellished) repetition, sequence, and recurrence.

Simple harmonic accompaniment may be added, at the discretion of the teacher.

CHAPTER XXXIV.

MELODIC EXPRESSION. CONCLUSION.

125. As stated in the Preface, the foregoing is a course of systematic exercise in melody *invention*, only,—not melody conception. For the latter there is, and should be, no other guide than the individual impulses of the maturing composer, founded upon, and controlled by, such natural and correct *habits of melodic thought* as he may have been fortunate enough to establish in early youth.

The transition from invention into conception is signalized by the increasing assertion of personal *emotional* impulses (*feeling*, as distinguished from thought), through which the element called Expression is instilled into the otherwise purely mechanical product, and the distinctions of Style, both individual and general, are created.

126. The presence of this element of Expression is manifested by an independent inclination to discriminate between the following attributes of musical style:—

(a) Between the major and minor *Modes*;—the latter of which is more passionate and sombre, the former brighter and more vigorous in effect, as a common rule.

(b) Between the duple and triple species of fundamental *Rhythm*;—the former more sturdy, the latter more graceful.

(c) Between rapid and slow *Tempo*, or degree of fundamental motion. This distinction influences, somewhat, even the technical formation of the melodic sentence,—in slow, or moderate, *tempi*, there is likely to be more *scale* than chord-derivation; considerable ornamentation is appropriate and necessary, and much — even extreme — diversity of tone-values is possible. On the contrary, in more active or rapid *tempi*, *chord*-derivation is apt to predominate over scale-derivation, though rapid scale-passages (as embellishment by passing-notes) are by no means infrequent; less ornamentation is likely to appear, and diversity of time-values is more limited, i. e., the rhythm is more nearly uniform.

(d) Between such conventional *Styles* as distinguish one class of composition from another (i. e., the Waltz from the Nocturne, the March from the Barcarolle, etc.). These are subject to no other laws than those of convention, or popular usage, and are best learned by observation.

127. All of these general qualities of melodic conception demand the more advanced discipline of musical Form, and can therefore be exercised only experimentally and briefly, at the discretion of the teacher, in the present course of melodic practice.

VOCAL SETTING

128. The most natural and wholesome artificial stimulus of definite and significant Expression in melody-invention, is that afforded by the *vocal setting*, or "*melodizing*," of a line or stanza of text. The simply mechanical endeavor to follow and confirm, as closely as possible, the varying shades of poetic and prosodic (or declamatory) expression of the given text, is calculated to arouse and develop the student's individual sense of Expression, and prepare for its untrammeled operation in the domain of *absolute* (instrumental) music.

129. The details of melodic effects, which find their parallels in the undulations of poetic expression, may be described approximately as follows:

(a) An *ascending* succession of tones, along the scale-line, indicates, ordinarily, an *increase* of emotional tension, or emphasis, a *descending* succession, *relaxation*.

(b) The effect of *step-wise* progressions is that of *gradual and smooth* change,—increase or decrease of the degree or stress of feeling. Whereas, when the tones progress in *skips*, either way, these changes of feeling are more *abrupt and positive*, about in proportion to the size of the skips.

(c) The progression in *chromatic* tones is more *seductive or passionate*, as a rule, than diatonic (i. e., scale) successions, and usually in proportion to their speed.

(d) The changes in force indicated by *crescendo* and *diminuendo*, arouse exactly similar impressions of increasing or decreasing volume or emphasis of feeling, the extremes of *fortissimo* and *pianissimo* indicate, respectively, utmost power or *nearness*, and utmost gentleness or *remoteness*.

(e) Sudden changes of force (*abrupt forte* or *piano* effects) corroborate swift, perhaps violent, impulses of emotion, these may be emphasized by simultaneous sudden changes of register or pitch,—i e, wide skips, the effect of which, as stated at *b*, is similarly abrupt and vigorous.

(f) The musical sense of a tone is powerfully influenced by its location and value in the rhythmic group. If it be placed upon the *accented* beat, or if its time-value be increased, such musical meaning as it possesses (absolute or comparative), is brought out with corresponding force. And, on the other hand, its location upon an *unaccented* beat, or its contraction to a brief time-value, diminishes the effect and value of its musical meaning.

(g) The definition of tonal meanings, and the bearing of the above upon them, may be roughly stated thus

The chord-root is powerful; the chord-third sweeter and more flexible; the chord-fifth soft and tender If placed upon the accented beats, or lengthened, they impart these respective qualities to the entire rhythmic group in which they occur.

The chord-7th and 9th, and the suspensions, are keen, conspicuous, and even obtrusive (in proportion to the degree of their dissonance); if accented, their effect is heightened; if prolonged, the effect of strain or tension is created. Appoggiaturas are similar, but usually still more pronounced in effect.

These, and other, distinctions may be tested in the melodic examples given in this book, some of which should be reviewed with special reference to the quality of Expression.

130. The principal rules of vocal setting are:

I. That the rhythmic details in the melody should agree closely with the prosodic effects of the text; i. e., accented syllables and important words should be set to the *comparatively* accented, higher, or longer, tones; and, vice versa, unaccented syllables and unimportant words should be set to comparatively unaccented, lower, or shorter, tones.

II. That the emotional contents of the text should be corroborated, by consistent employment of the distinctions of melodic expression above explained.

III. That notes set to separate words or syllables must be detached, in notation; while two or more notes set to one word or syllable must be connected, either by beam, tie, or slur.

The following examples briefly illustrate these rules. The pupil may find numerous others, in *English* Oratorios, Cantatas, Anthems and Songs (i. e., composed originally to English words):

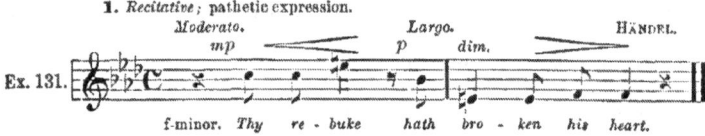

LESSON 35.

The melodic setting of lines, and of brief stanzas, from church hymn-books; or from the Psalms and other parts of the Bible; or from secular poetic writings. At first, a few exercises in *Recitative* form, i. e., not strictly metrical. Afterwards, very numerous studies in metrical Phrase, Period, or Double-period form.

After correction and approval by the teacher, they may be harmonized, or provided with a simple instrumental accompaniment.

THE END.

TABLE OF CONTENTS.

DIVISION ONE.

ESSENTIAL TONES.

	PAGE
CHAPTER I. ....MAJOR. THE SCALE-LINE, REGULAR	5
First Primary Rule	5
The Four-measure Phrase....	7
CHAPTER II. ....THE MAJOR SCALE-LINE, EXCEPTIONAL................ ...	10
CHAPTER III. ....THE CHORD-LINE......	12
Second Primary Rule	12
Fundamental Harmonic Principles	13
Rules for Single Skips.	15
CHAPTER IV.........THE CHORD-LINE, CONTINUED.	19
Summary of Rules (par. 39)	24
Miscellaneous Illustrations (Ex 36)	25
CHAPTER V... ...... MINOR..	28
CHAPTER VI........ DIVERSITY OF RHYTHM, REGULAR	31
CHAPTER VII ...... .THE PERIOD-FORM	34
CHAPTER VIII. .....IRREGULAR RHYTHM....	36
CHAPTER IX. ....EXCEPTIONAL SEMICADENCES	40
CHAPTER X. . ..... SYNTAX OF MELODY	41
Repetition and Sequence, Exact....................	41
CHAPTER XI ....SYNTAX OF MELODY, CONTINUED	44
Repetition and Sequence, Modified	44
CHAPTER XII........SYNTAX OF MELODY, CONTINUED	49
Application to the Period-form.......................	49
CHAPTER XIII..... .ALTERED SCALE-STEPS, MAJOR	51
CHAPTER XIV. ......ALTERED SCALE-STEPS, MINOR	55
CHAPTER XV. ......MODULATION, OR CHANGES OF KEY	58
CHAPTER XVI. .... .MODULATION, CONTINUED...	62
Transient Modulations	62

TABLE OF CONTENTS.

		PAGE
Chapter XVII.	Modulation, Continued.	63
	Application to Period-form.	63
Chapter XVIII.	Modulation, Chromatic.	65
Chapter XIX.	Modulation, Continued.	66
	Overlapping Scale-lines.	66
Chapter XX.	Modulation in Sequences, and at Cadences.	68
Chapter XXI.	Chromatic Melody.	70
Chapter XXII.	The Double-period Form.	72

DIVISION TWO.

UNESSENTIAL, OR EMBELLISHING, TONES.

Chapter XXIII.	Definition of Distinction between Essential and Unessential Tones.	75
	The Suspension.	76
Chapter XXIV.	The Anticipation.	79
Chapter XXV.	The Passing-note (single).	81
Chapter XXVI.	The Passing-note (successive).	83
	Chromatic Passing-note.	84
	Repeated Passing-note.	86
Chapter XXVII.	Neighboring-Notes.	87
Chapter XXVIII.	Neighboring-notes, Continued.	92
Chapter XXIX.	Neighboring-note as Appoggiatura.	96
Chapter XXX.	Double-appoggiatura.	100
Chapter XXXI.	Appoggiatura, Continued.	105
	Unresolved Neighboring-note.	106
Chapter XXXII.	Evolution of Melodic Germs.	109
Chapter XXXIII.	Melodic Evolution, Continued.	115
	Disguised Recurrences.	115
Chapter XXXIV.	Melodic Expression.	121
	Vocal Setting.	122

CPSIA information can be obtained
at www.ICGtesting.com
Printed in the USA
BVHW010205110322
631229BV00002B/44